play like

Keith Moon

The Ultimate Drum Lesson

Audio Access Included!

PLAYBACK+
Speed • Pitch • Balance • Loop

by *Andy Ziker*

To access audio visit:
www.halleonard.com/mylibrary

Enter Code
2298-5497-3794-6335

Photo © Trinifold Archive

ISBN 978-1-4950-2830-4

HAL•LEONARD®
7777 W. BLUEMOUND RD. P.O. BOX 13819 MILWAUKEE, WI 53213

Visit Hal Leonard Online at
www.halleonard.com

CONTENTS

INTRODUCTION

Keith Moon might be best known for his loony behavior with the Who—one of the most iconic rock bands of the '60s and '70s. He pushed drum kits off risers, trashed hotel rooms, and over-indulged in drugs and alcohol (which unfortunately led to his untimely death). Though here we're mostly concerned about Moon's groundbreaking drumming, you can't completely separate his onstage performance from his offstage behavior. A deeper look into his character and influences—followed by transcriptions, analyses, and lessons—is the first step in understanding this one-of-a-kind musician.

Personality

According to his teachers and classmates, the young Moon had inexhaustible energy and became a class clown. His ability as a mimic was legendary. "He could vacuum a character off someone in ten minutes and he would then become them. Not just a caricature, he'd get inside. It was scary!" said Roger Daltrey, lead singer of the Who. Though he showed promise in English and science, he learned at an early age that music was his calling. In fact, Moon negotiated a mutual separation between himself and Alperton, the school he was attending, at age 15. "I didn't mind. I hated school," Moon said. He tried boxing, drums, bugle (in the Sea Cadet Corps), and experimented with science kits, but he hit his mark when he sat down at the drum set. "I found out that I could not do anything else. I tried several things, and this was the only one I enjoyed doing." Drumming soon became an extension of his personality.

According to Bob Henrit—Moon's friend and a drummer with Argent and The Kinks—"Moon the Loon" was able to maintain control and function on the drums (though with his famous reckless abandon) because he was "crazy in a productive way." Moon also had a caring, sensitive side to his personality as evidenced by his relationship late in life with his godson, Zak Starkey (son of Ringo Starr). As Zak put it in an interview with *Modern Drummer*: "When my brother, sister, and I used to stay with my dad there, we would occasionally spend a few days at Keith's house. Keith was the babysitter. We would just hang out and talk about anything, really—girls, surfing, bands, drums. He wasn't crazy in any way, except for that look in his eye."

Though known as one of the world's top attention-getting showmen (stick spinning and tossing, flamboyant clothing, hilarious stage banter, standing on his kit, setting off explosions, and much more), Moon insisted on playing on the stage floor (not on a riser) with his bandmates. He was committed to just being one of the guys, and this also drove his playing style. Moon made a career out of reacting to what was happening around him. Starkey says, "He read music perfectly, through listening," and Henrit adds, "The Who were the sum of their parts. They worked because they were so diverse. They just went for it and enjoyed themselves."

Nature Vs. Nurture

Because Moon developed into such a natural, unorthodox player, it's easy to assume that he sat down at the drums one day as a youngster and immediately began playing at a high level. In reality, Moon began taking lessons in 1961 at the age of 15 with Carlo Little, the drummer of a popular area rock group known as Screaming Lord Sutch and the Savages. Little had a loud, aggressive style featuring a cannon of a kick foot. Moon emulated his tutor, practiced intently, and learned the fundamentals but expanded on them to suit his rapidly developing style.

Moon once said, "I didn't actually listen to drummers. I listened to riffs and I play riffs on drums." This wasn't exactly the whole truth. He went out to hear Little many times and also frequented a number of establishments to absorb what he could from other local drummers. Moon also spent countless hours at home listening to records of his favorite stickmen: Eric Delaney and Gene Krupa (big band jazz), Hal Blaine and Dennis Wilson (surf music), and Ginger Baker, DJ Fontana, and Bob Henrit (rock). He told *Drum & Drumming*, "My whole style of drumming changed when I joined the band. Before, I had just been copying straight from records, but with the Who, I had to develop a style of my own."

Moon eventually rejected the notion of practicing and supposedly only practiced before tours and when he rehearsed with the Who. Though Moon kept a kit at each of his homes, he only bashed around from time to time. "I don't practice on my own. As far as we go, as long as we have the bare bones of a song, that's the way we rehearse. It's just to get the bones, the verses, solos, and the general framework of the song. Then, within that framework, we're free to experiment. It's rather like plasticine; you've got the thing there, but it's malleable. You can actually shape it and stretch it but you're still left with what you started out with."

Who Are You?

Moon developed more than enough technique to express himself. Once he joined forces with bandmates who trusted each other, he was free to allow his instincts to take over. It's because of this, according to Henrit, that you're unlikely to become the next Moon: "No one can play like Keith, and no one is ever going to. Simon Phillips (one of Moon's replacements in the Who) came close. He had the technique, but he was thinking it, while Moonie wasn't thinking it. He was just experiencing it."

Though this may seem to quash any need to study the materials in this book—and is probably not a selling point— this is essentially true about studying the style of any drummer or musician. It's unlikely that you'll end up sounding exactly like Moon, but you can definitely incorporate bits and pieces of his style into your own playing. After all, Moon himself borrowed from other drummers to develop his craft.

Before you dive into the transcriptions, analyses, and lessons (not to mention an extensive chapter on Moon's gear), consider this: Though many of his greatest performances are from Who shows—such as *Live at Leeds*—the material examined here is almost all from studio albums. This way, when you refer back to the original songs, sound clarity will provide you with the most ideal learning experience.

Following is a summary of the content in the book. If you take your time and work your way carefully through each chapter, your bandmates and audiences will soon thank you. Every drummer needs some Keith Moon in their playing.

Set-Up

Moon's first kit with the Who was a basic four-piece, but his taste for a full pallet of sounds caused his later kits to eventually grow to 17 pieces. This not only affected his overall sound, but it caused drummers all over the world to desire bigger set-ups.

Songs

Five classic Who songs are analyzed and broken down into digestible lessons, and then each song is transcribed note-for-note with lyrics included to help you keep your place. The accompanying audio includes full band tracks (with drums).

Essential Grooves

Though he often blurs the line between groove and drum solo, a close examination shows a method behind Moon's madness. Here, seven of his all-time greatest grooves are held up to the magnifying glass.

Essential Fills/Solos

This section is chock-full of Moon's improvisations—both fills and solos. These licks are carefully dissected from six songs, showing how Moon walks a tightrope between functionality and art.

Stylistic DNA

Here we take a look at aspects of Moon's playing that produce his stylistic fingerprint. Mini-lessons enable you to assimilate his skills and concepts into your playing.

Must Hear

Listening with a critical ear is probably the best way to tap into another drummer's style. An essential discography of both Moon's influences and performances are listed here.

Must See

Luckily for us, the Who is one of the most filmed rock 'n' roll bands in history. Essential video examples (including those from YouTube) of Moon's playing are included, along with clips of drummers who have since attempted to take over the reins.

ABOUT THE AUDIO

To access the audio examples that accompany this book, simply go to www.halleonard.com/mylibrary and enter the code found on page 1. This will grant you instant access to each example. Look for audio icons sprinkled throughout the book. When you click on each example, the audio player gives you control over tempo, pitch, balance, and looping.

SET-UP

When his father Alf bought him his first drum kit at the age of 15, Moon was already passionate about drums. The moment he and his friend Gerry Evans set up the kit in Moon's home, he "attacked them like a madman." As soon as Moon began to play in front of audiences, his kit became more than a musical instrument—he used it as a medium for his own brand of performance art.

Exotic finishes, unusual configurations and instrument choices, and innovative hardware solutions are all part of the history of Moon's kits, now adored by collectors around the world. Ironically, his drums are cherished even though often in bad condition (from self-inflicted wounds). Maybe that's the charm in it—his drums played an active role in the show.

Drumkits

Early Period (Single Bass)

- **Premier Blue Pearl four-piece (1961–64)**: His father paid 15 quid up front for the first kit, and Moon paid the rest himself through installments. It was bought from Paramount Music, West End of London, and the deal was secured by Moon's friend, Gerry Evans. In the early '60s, this was the standard outfit for drummers, who, for the most part, had not yet ventured into using more pieces than this. John Entwistle, bass player for the Who, remembers how the kit was tied all together with a huge coil of rope. "We couldn't understand why until he went into a drum solo, and everything started to sway backwards and forwards."

  Drums
  > Bass drum: 14" x 20"
  > Rack tom: 8" x 12"
  > Floor tom: 20" x 16"
  > Snare: unknown

- **Ludwig Super Classic Black Oyster Pearl four-piece (1964–65)**: Moon used this kit on the British TV rock/pop show, *Ready, Steady, Go*. Performing on TV in the mid-'60s was all about miming. Moon took a silly approach to this and didn't take much care in getting the drum parts right. The drums were quite fragile from this period. "If you weren't careful, they would break around the casings. You couldn't throw them around," says Henrit.

  Drums
  > Bass drum: 22"
  > Rack tom: 13"
  > Floor tom: 16"
  > Snare: 14" Supraphonic 400

  Cymbals
  > Avedis Zildjian
  > 20" ride
  > 18" crash
  > 14" hi-hats

- **Ludwig Super Classic Silver Sparkle five-piece (1965)**
  Drums
  > Bass drum: 22"
  > Rack tom: 13"
  > Floor tom: 14"
  > Floor tom: 16"
  > Snare: 14" Supraphonic 400

  Cymbals
  > Avedis Zildjian
  > 20" ride
  > 18" crash
  > 14" hi-hats

  Stands
  > Rogers Swiv-O-Matic

- **Premier Red Sparkle six-piece (1965)**: Moon received this kit at the start of an endorsement deal with Premier, beginning a longstanding relationship with the company. He was one of the first rock drummers to use two mounted toms, though he didn't come up with the idea. (Louie Bellson convinced Gretsch Drums to do this back in 1946.) Rack mounts weren't meant for rock playing at this time, so Moon persuaded Premier to come up with stronger, more durable hardware.

  Henrit remembers years later playing this kit for Roger Daltrey's first solo album. The sessions were at Daltrey's studio in Sussex, and he fell in love with the idea of two mounted toms. "I had never had that before and have used two mounted toms ever since."
  Drums
  > Bass drum: 22"
  > Floor tom: 16" x 16"
  > Floor tom: 16" x 20"
  > Toms: Two 14" x 8"
  > Snare: 14" x 5.5" Premier 2000

  Cymbals
  > Unknown make
  > 20" ride
  > 18" crash
  > 14" hi-hats

Middle Period (Double Bass)

- **Premier Red Sparkle nine-piece (1966)**: Moon added to his six-piece kit, and it featured two bass drums locked together with tom mounts. The kit initially had two 14" x 8" tom toms, but he later switched to three, precipitating an unusual hardware solution: placing the mount on the left-side bass drum farther down the drum. This allowed for the three toms to be equally spaced apart. A third floor tom—set up on his left—was usually used for set lists, sticks, drinks, and towels.

  Moon was undoubtedly influenced by two of his favorite big band drummers: double-bass pioneers Louie Bellson and London's Eric Delaney. Moon may have been further talked into the idea by Ginger Baker, who allegedly told Moon about ordering a two-bass kit from Ludwig. Also, Phil Wainman, drummer for one of the Who's support groups, Jimmy Cliff Sound, used two bass drums. Moon may have felt upstaged by Wainman and pressured to make the move to another kick.
  Drums
  > Bass drums: Two 22"
  > Floor toms (three): 16" x 16" and often one 20" x 16"
  > Toms (three): 14" x 8"
  > Snare: 14" x 5.5" Premier 2000

  Cymbals
  Paiste & Zildjian
  > 14" or 15" hi-hats (usually not used on stage)
  > Two 16" crashes
  > 20" ride

- **Premier "Pictures of Lily" nine-piece custom (1967–69)**: Premier custom-built at least three of what became his best-known kits. Moon himself came up with the idea to incorporate "Pictures of Lily" into the design, a novel idea because no one had ever printed custom graphics onto a drum shell before. The image was based on a postcard from the '20s of a Vaudeville pinup. The artwork was pasted on to the shell and then clear-coated. According to Moon, the "Pictures of Lily" kit took six months to complete. It was also known as "Keith Moon, Patent British Exploding Drummer," as the phrase was interspersed throughout. The wrap was glow-in-the-dark but, for whatever reason, was never shown under black light. Premier went on to make the kit available to the public.

  Drums
    Bass drums: Two 22" x 14"
    Floor toms (three): Two 16" x 18" and one 16" x 16"
    Toms (three): 14" x 8"
    Snare: 14" x 5.5"

  Cymbals
    Paiste & Zildjian
    14" hi-hats (usually not used on stage)
    16" crash
    20" ride

- **Premier Champagne Silver nine-piece custom (1968–70)**
  Drums and Cymbals: Same as the Pictures of Lily kit.

- **Zickos Acrylic ten-piece (1970–71)**: Keith bought a transparent acrylic drum kit from Zickos drum company during the 1970 US tour. Several weeks later, he ordered another one. The quality of acrylic drums was poor at this time, producing shells that were not particularly pleasing to the ears. Moon said, "I got it in the States. I have never got a good sound with it. Visually is all I got it for, for television and miming." [*Drums & Drumming*] Henrit remarked, "He would fill them with water and fish. None of the plexiglass kits are really strong. It's the same stuff that they used for the front window in airplane cockpits."

  Drums
    Bass drums (two): 22" x 18"
    Floor toms (two): 18" x 18"
    Floor toms (two): 18" x 16"
    Toms (two): 14" x 10"
    Tom: 14" x 7"
    Snare: 14" x 7"

- **Premier Black nine-piece custom (1971–73)**: Included metal plates inside and custom "iron cross" metal plates on the exteriors of the bass drums for added strength.
  Drums and Cymbals: Same as the Pictures of Lily kit.

Late Period

- **Premier Double Tom Row 12-piece (1973–74)**: This monster came in both black and gold finishes and featured two rows of toms: one row of double-headed toms (closest to Moon) and one row of single-headed toms (also known as concert toms). Moon had so many targets that his friends began to refer to him as "the Octopus." Henrit recalls, "It gave him more to hit. It wasn't like he hit a particular drum to get a sound that very millisecond. He hit it because he was doing a fill that went all the way around the toms and maybe back again."

  Drums
  > Bass drums (two): 22" x 14"
  > Floor tom: 18" x 16"
  > Floor tom: 16" x 16"
  > Concert tom: 16" x 16"
  > Concert tom: 15" x 12"
  > Concert tom: 14" x 10"
  > Concert tom: 13" x 9"
  > Toms (three): 14" x 8"
  > Snare: 14" x 5.5" or 6.5"

  Cymbals
  > Paiste 2002 series
  > 14" hi-hats
  > 18" crash
  > 20" crash
  > 20" rides

- **Premier Cream White 14-piece (1975–76)**: Moon requested gold-plated hardware, but Premier advised against this because of rapid wear. They used copper instead. This kit actually has three rows of toms on the right side of the kit: two floor toms, two concert toms, and two timbales.

  Moon gifted the kit on to Ringo Starr, who in turn gave it to his son Zak Starkey. Starkey recalls, "It was a double bass drum kit with eleven toms. I was twelve then, and we lived in a village called Winkfield, Berkshire. The big Premier set was very safe. It was like having a wall all around you. No one can see me, but everyone could hear me, including our neighbors, who were trying to stop me from playing drums. I could reach all the drums, and within a year I was playing gigs with that kit." [*Modern Drummer*]

  Drums
  > Bass drums (two): 22"
  > Floor tom: 18"
  > Floor tom: 16" x 16"
  > Concert tom: 16" x 18"
  > Concert tom: 15" x 12"
  > Concert tom: 14" x 10"
  > Concert tom: 13" x 9"
  > Concert tom: 12" x 8"
  > Toms (three): 14" x 10"
  > Timbales (two)
  > Snare: 14" x 5.5" or 6.5" Gretsch

  Cymbals
  > Paiste 2002 series
  > 14" hi-hats
  > 14" splash
  > 18" crash
  > 20" crash
  > 22" ride

- **Premier Final 16-piece (1977–78)**: His final stage kit, used for his last two shows, was finished in chrome steel over a birch shell. Moon felt that his set-up finally allowed him to handle everything the Who could throw at him. "I can cover from a roar with the timpani right up to the smallest timbale…That's why I have so many drums onstage because, with the Who, there's Pete who plays a lot of chords and John who plays very intricate bass figures that I work with, and we have this empathy between us." [*International Musician and Recording World*]

> **Drums**
> > Bass drums (two): 22"
> > Floor tom: 18"
> > Floor tom: 16"
> > Concert toms (six): 10", 12", 13", 14", 15", and 16"
> > Toms (three): 14" x 10"
> > Timbales (two)
> > Snare: 14" x 5.5" or 6.5"
>
> **Cymbals**
> > Mostly Paiste 2002 series
> > 14" hi-hats
> > 14" splash (Zildjian)
> > 18" crash
> > 20" crash
> > 22" ride (Zildjian)

- **Premier Natural Single Bass 17-piece (1978)**: This kit was used in the studio in 1978 and for a special version of "Who Are You," filmed for *The Kids Are Alright*. (Note: the sizes/dimensions for this kit are unknown.)

  > **Drums**
  > > Bass drum
  > > Concert toms (10)
  > > Toms (three)
  > > Floor toms (two)
  > > Snare
  >
  > **Cymbals**
  > > Hi-hats (Paiste Sound Edge)
  > > Ride (Zildjian)
  > > Crashes (two Paiste)
  > > China

What If

At the time of Moon's passing in the late '70s, drum and cymbal companies dove headfirst into a period of innovation that is still ongoing. Though Moon only caught a glimpse of this, he had already become excited about many new products and the sounds they could produce. It's easy to wonder about what direction Moon was going to go next.

- **Staccato**: In 1978, Moon was enthralled with these strange-looking, horn-shaped fiberglass drums, and a partnership was agreed upon only days before his untimely death. Henrit says, "When I was in The Kinks, one of our security guys had a drum company called Staccato. They were like North drums, but the British version. The fiberglass would have stood up to what Moonie was doing better than what Premier made."

- **Syndrums and Electronic Percussion**: According to historian Martin Forsbom, Moon was curious about electronic drums and the possibility of making new sounds in the future. Henrit, who owned a drum store at the time that Moon frequented, carried electronic drums called Syndrums but doesn't remember selling any to Moon. "I don't think they would have been his scene. I think he would have trashed those things in no time at all. He could have easily had a Simmons drum kit, and I would have been happy to get one for him."

- **Snares on Each Drum**: Moon once told Henrit about the idea of putting snares (metal strands) on each drum (including the toms). Interestingly enough, this is a technique still used today by iconic drummer Jim Keltner, who also happened to be one of Moon's friends.

- **Cymbal Types and Other Sounds**: In Moon's later set-ups, you'll notice that he had a huge variety of drums but, in comparison, a modest number of cymbals. With the improvements in cymbal stand design and the advent of racks, he would have undoubtedly enjoyed having had a whole battery of effects cymbals, cymbal stacks, and remote hi-hats.

More on Hardware

- **Strength**: Mick Double, Moon's long-time drum tech, went to great lengths to adapt the hardware to make it sturdier. Double used high-tensile stainless steel bolts in Moon's Premier 250 bass drum pedals to prevent damage with the bass drum heads. He also anchored the drums heavily to the ground, because Moon had a habit of standing on top of the toms.

- **Cymbal Stands**: Moon's cymbal stands changed as the technology improved. He originally used straight stands with flush (or flat) bases, but his later kits used booms and the same tripod design popular today.

- **Tom Mounts**: Moon used a standard Premier "oval post" tom mounting block on his Premier Natural Single Bass kit. These were prone to crack by far less lethal hitters, and so Moon switched to Roger's Swiv-O-Matic, which were the best mounts made during the '60s.

- **Bass Pedals**: Moon used a Premier 250 pedal.

Orchestral and Latin Percussion

- **Symphonic Gong**: Moon added this piece starting with the Premier Double Tom Row kits.

- **Timpani**: The timpani arrived beginning with the Champagne Silver kit in 1969.

Moon: "Oh yes, I've just got a set of timps. You know, those huge drums people like Eric Delaney use. They're made by Premier and give a tremendous 'lift' to songs. I won't use them in many numbers; that would spoil the effect. I haven't tried them on record yet, but the time will come." [*Beat Instrumental*, 1967]

- **Timbales**: These were added beginning with his Premier Cream White 14-piece.

- **Clave**: This was used prominently used on "Magic Bus."

More on Cymbals

Even though Moon mostly used one brand of drums (Premier), his choice of cymbals oscillated for many years. He mostly played Paiste, but sometimes went with Zildjian. Late in his career, Moon signed an endorsement deal with Zildjian. Eddie Haynes, who worked with Zildjian at the time, recalls Moon saying that, until Zildjian reached out, no cymbal manufacturer had ever bothered to ask him about endorsing their cymbals.

Moon's use of the hi-hat evolved throughout his career. During the instrumental section of "Anyway, Anyhow, Anywhere" (1965), he keeps the beat on the hi-hat (similar to a jazz drummer) and plays ferocious drum rolls over the top of the hi-hat pulse. Moon abandoned the hi-hat completely—removing it from his set-up—during many of the Who's live performances. This occurred around the time of his switch from single to double bass. Moon inserted a large crash in its stead, and the resulting timekeeping wash became a characteristic part of his sound. When Moon began using the hi-hat again, he would often set it to slightly open, but can be heard controlling it—in a more typical manner—on *Who Are You* in 1978.

More on Snares

Besides an assortment of Premier snares, Moon also used Ludwig and Gretsch.

- **Gretsch DRB Special**: Moon used these drums in 1971. Henrit tells the story of his introduction to the now famous drum: "We did a gig with the Who in Rotterdam. The Eagles were also on the bill; they had just come out and were doing a European tour. I went into Moon's dressing room, and he was sitting in his favorite arm chair, which the crew took everywhere. He had a snare drum. This snare drum has become the holy grail. It was called the DRB Special, a worn-out Gretsch that was breathed on by someone named DRB. Nobody, including me, knows who DRB is. I didn't take the DRB Special. I still don't know where it comes from. I think it has something to do with Frank Ippolito's Professional Percussion Center in NYC in the '60s."

Headphones

Moon used headphones on stage starting in 1971 to hear the backing tape of synthesizer parts on songs such as "Baba O'Riley" and "Won't Get Fooled Again." He used gaffers tape to keep them from falling off his head. "The big problem was not being able to hear the tape [programmed synth]. So we've got John and Pete blasting away and this tape, which is important because they take their thing off of me," said Moon.

Drumsticks

Moon used Premier Ajax C and Ajax E, which were both sticks that he found to be durable. He flipped the stick (left hand only) when playing rimshots on the snare and intermittently positioned his pointer finger on top of the stick, unusual when riding on a crash. Henrit elaborates: "Not only is it difficult to bounce [the tip of the stick off of a surface] that way, but it hurts. There's a lot of video examples where he's miming and playing like that, but he might be putting us all on as well. Winding everyone up fifty years later to say, 'Look how I was playing.'" Moon also used mallets on *Tommy*.

Drumheads

Moon mostly used Premier Everplay Extra drumheads—smooth white, almost transparent, one-ply plastic heads. He sometimes used Ludwig heads and put Remo CS Black Dot Clears on his toms.

Tuning

Henrit recalls that, in the '60s, tuning wasn't an exact science as it is today. You only really thought about it if a wrinkle appeared or if you had to replace a broken head. Bob Pridden, the Who's longtime soundman, remembers Moon spending a lot of time tuning the kit. "He tuned the skins very tight. They were very percussive and bell-like. Before drums were miked up, Pete and John's rigs were so loud, Keith had to be loud to get up over it all. That tuning did cut through. If it was tuned down low, it would never get over or cut through that noise on stage."

When Moon used three rack toms of the same size (on his double-kick kits), he tuned them from high to low (left to right).

Miking

Pridden first tried miking each individual drum, which sounded "dreadful." He then discovered the Glyn Johns technique, which he learned from Johns himself, and was then able to capture the true Moon sound. Pridden explains, "Two U87s brought in at a certain angle: one over the top and one coming in from the side, maybe a snare drum mike, and a bass drum mike (or two). That was it. The drums breathed. With an acoustic instrument, you never stick your ear right into it, do you?"

Destruction

Moon's aggression towards his instrument wasn't really his idea to begin with. During one performance, Pete Townsend accidentally decapitated his guitar because of a low ceiling, and Moon immediately reacted to it. Pridden explains further, "There was nowhere else to go at the end of a whole show. The only way to end it was to smash everything, because we didn't like doing encores. Keith followed suit, and it really helped us. The Who rarely played an encore because there was no equipment left."

With a few exceptions, most of the damage Moon did to his drums was limited to broken heads and torn drum wraps. Depending on who you talk to, Moon either planned ahead to minimize the damage or went all out to destroy them. Nevertheless, after the dust settled, the drums somehow seemed to be in repairable condition.

NOTE: A special thanks to Martin Forsborm for compiling information about Moon's gear for the website, WhoTabs. Forsborm's work became an invaluable resource for the "Set-Up" chapter in this book. (He also gave input for the "Must See" and "Must Hear" chapters near the back of the book.) Make sure to check out WhoTabs to discover even more detailed information about Moon's set-ups.

SONGS

The following five songs were chosen very carefully, considering factors such as production quality, performance, and the potential to learn Moon's style and technique. As mentioned previously, you may want to also check out the Who's live recordings, such as *Live at Leeds* (1970). The Who has always been known for their on-stage performances, and Moon was at the top of his game during that show.

Pinball Wizard
From *Tommy*, 1969

"Kit Lambert producing. Keith was blossoming then, because we were playing lots of gigs. A live working band." [Pridden]

"Pinball Wizard" was released as a single before the rock opera album *Tommy* came out, reaching #4 in the UK charts. Moon's intuitive drum parts were groundbreaking at the time and still stand up today as one of rock drumming's all-time great performances. His grooves and fills fit like puzzle pieces with Townsend, Daltrey, and Entwhistle.

Intro and First Verse

As the song begins, Townsend plays a 16-bar intro on acoustic guitar (and overdubbed electric), leading into the first verse, which adds Daltrey's vocals and Entwistle's syncopated bass line. The drums arrive in bar 25, a full measure before most typical drummers would dare enter. Notice how the one-bar drum fill weaves in and out of the vocal melody and how Moon frames the word "plays" by leaving space on beat 2 in measure 25.

Moon doesn't plan out his fills; he reacts to what's going on around him and trusts his intuition. The following exercise will allow you to experience the mostly uniform two-bar structure taken from the end of each verse in "Pinball Wizard," which Moon uses four times in the song. This exercise repeats the groove/fill from measure 36 and then one-bar fills from measures 25, 37, 59, and 85.

Pinball Wizard
Example 1

As he gets into the verse groove (measure 26), four things are apparent:
* Moon is back to using the hi-hat (during live performances around this time, he had abandoned the hi-hat altogether).
* He has a penchant for using four-stroke ruffs played as 16th-note triplets (in the first verse and the outro on the 2 + of just about every measure).
* He interjects crash cymbal hits in unexpected spots (here, quite often on the 3 +).
* He uses buzz strokes with his left hand on the snare (located here on the second 16th-note triplet of the 2 +).

Though Moon rarely repeated ideas for very long, here, one four-stroke ruff orchestration is used to create this exercise. Instead of landing on the 2 + only, as done in source measure 32, the rudiment is played in every eighth-note location.

Pinball Wizard
Example 2

As mentioned previously, Moon liked to use off-beat crashes in unusual locations. In this exercise, a crash cymbal placed on the 3 + is included in four common rock patterns. Notice that the snare following the crash is played without a hi-hat.

Pinball Wizard
Example 3

The last half of measure 36 is a straightforward fill (eighths and 16ths on the snare) with consecutive bass drum eighth notes played underneath. Then, in measure 37, only one bass drum is used (with crash cymbal) on the downbeat at the beginning of a syncopated fill around the drums. The lack of additional bass drum helps to underscore the vocal phrase, "sure plays a mean pinball," and provides a contrast in timbre to measure 36.

First Chorus

This section (measures 42–47) is chock-full of Moon-isms: buzz strokes, four-stroke ruff combinations on the 2 + and 4 +, and continuous double-bass (either a single- or double-bass). He uses open hi-hats—most of them played in two or three consecutive eighth-note locations. Notice how these openings support lyrical phrases such as "to be a twist" in measure 43, though Moon sticks with the idea, building momentum all the way through the chorus.

Similar to the first two measures of the first chorus (measures 42–43), in this exercise, one measure of a rock pattern with continuous single bass is followed by a measure of the same pattern with continuous, simultaneous double-bass. You will need to move your left foot from the hi-hat in the first measure to the left-side bass drum (or pedal) in the second measure.

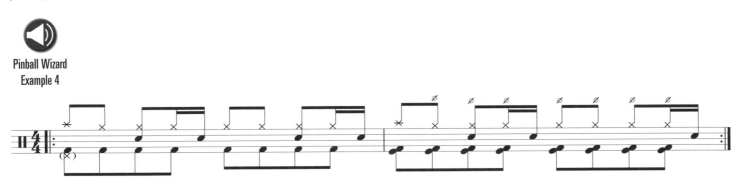

Pinball Wizard
Example 4

NOTE: At this point in his career, Moon set the top and bottom hi-hat cymbals very close to one another. This way he could create a tight, closed sound by applying a small amount of pressure to the pedalboard, a sloshy sound by letting his foot rest on the pedalboard without pressing down, or a somewhat open sound by removing his foot entirely from the pedal. The latter allowed him to still keep his right hand playing time on the hi-hat when his left foot moved to the second bass drum. He could even produce a slight chick sound if needed.

Bridge

Moon welcomes chances to express himself, especially if given a wide-open space such as the one-measure fill in measure 51. Three-note groupings demarcated by the snare are followed by Moon's musical go-to punctuation mark: the four-stroke ruff. Check out how Moon plays half-open and open hi-hats on the 1 +, 2, and 3, giving the fill a three-dimensional effect.

Try It
Using *Playback+* from the accompanying online audio, loop the bridge (measure 48–51) from the full song version of "Pinball Wizard." Each time you reach the fourth measure, improvise a one-measure fill in the style of Moon: two three-note groupings of eighth-notes, ending with a four-stroke ruff.

Third Verse

Moon adds open hi-hat punctuations and crashes on the 1 + to the mix (starting in measure 52), ramping up the intensity yet another notch. In the final chorus (measure 64), the drums are now firing on all cylinders; open hi-hats, four-stroke ruffs, and continuous bass drum eighth notes drive us to the crash on beat 1 of the interlude.

The Big Picture

Whatever the inspiration behind Moon's drum parts on tunes such as "Pinball Wizard," the end result is absolute genius. Imitating his grooves and fills note-for-note is a great exercise; to take this imitation to another level, however, you have to try get inside his head. We've already examined how he accentuates Daltrey's vocal parts by using rhythmic density and sound source choices (including articulations). He not only reacts to the vocals, but Moon also listens and reacts to all of the instruments around him. The following will help you hear the song from the drummer's perspective.

- **Bass**: In "Pinball Wizard," as in most of the Who's music, Moon and Entwistle forge a symbiotic relationship. At times, the drums and bass are completely intertwined, such as during the second verse or first chorus. Other times, they separate from one another, such as during the four-bar instrumental section connecting the second verse to the first chorus. At that moment, Entwistle supports Townsend's electric guitar riff, and Moon takes an opportunity to play lead drums.

- **Acoustic Guitar (heard mostly on the right side of the mix)**: In each verse, Townsend outlines a four-against-three polyrhythm using accented 16ths. Moon contrasts this (and grounds it) with a driving eighth-note groove.

- **Electric Guitar**: Moon both supports and contrasts the offbeat guitar rhythms in each chorus. Moon's ability to juggle roles is one of the keys to the sound of the band.

PINBALL WIZARD

Words and Music by Peter Townshend

Bridge

How do you think _____ he does _____ it? (I don't _____ know.) _____

What makes him _____ so good? _____

Verse

3. Ain't got no dis - trac - tions, can't hear no buz -zers and bells. Don't

see no lights a flash - in', plays by sense of smell. _____

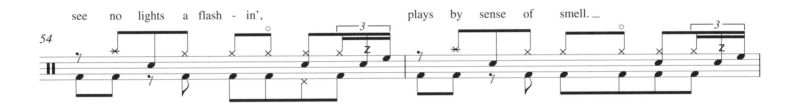

Al - ways gets a re - play, nev-er seen _____ him fall. _____ That

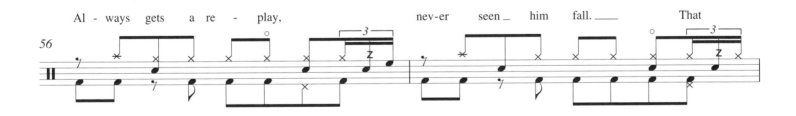

deaf, dumb, and blind _____ kid sure plays a mean pin - ball.

*Played on rim.

Won't Get Fooled Again
From *Who's Next*, 1971

"Glyn Johns was producing, which really helped. Still Keith. Slightly more controlled but fantastic." [Pridden]

"Once you start it and you're working with it, you've got to pull yourself in a bit. Be a bit stricter and tighter. The difficulty was when we first started using it, I tried to try to slightly increase the tempo where I felt it needed a lift and then bring it back, but of course you can't do that with a synthesizer. You're stuck with this metronome. When I felt I needed a lift, instead of speeding it up a bit, I'd change the sound of the drums by using something else. The effect would be there—the same as speeding up." [Moon, *International Musician* interview]

"See there, where the tempo started to die, how he picked it up? The man is a drummer." [Jazz great Elvin Jones referring to Moon during a blind listening test]

Attempting to supplant *Tommy* (1969), Pete Townsend began work on a futuristic rock opera that was to be called "Lifehouse." The project was derailed due to its complexity and the drug abuse by manager and producer, Kit Lambert. Fortunately, with the assistance of a different producer, Glyn Johns, the material was salvaged and transformed into a more typical studio album. In turn, *Who's Next* became one of the band's most successful records both in terms of sales and critical acclaim.

Who's Next was one of the first rock albums to combine man and the machine. A programmed synthesizer plays throughout "Won't Get Fooled Again," therefore tying Moon to a click track. Johns, already a well-respected studio presence at the time, demanded a more straightforward approach from the normally freewheeling drummer. Because of these constraints, Moon played more succinctly than usual, but no less creatively.

"Won't Get Fooled Again" was first released as a 3:36 single in the summer of 1971 and then later in the year as the final track of *Who's Next*, weighing in at an impressive 8:33.

Intro

After a 17-bar synth intro, Moon plays crash cymbal and double-kick along with Townsend's power chords on the downbeat of measure 18. This sets up a call-and-response from measure 18–21: a hit on beat 1 in the first measure, followed by syncopated eighths played by matching drums and bass in the second measure. Starting in measure 22, Moon plays one of the most recognizable four-bar drum phrases in rock history, featuring bass drum/middle tom on 3 and 3 + (measures 23–24), crash/snare on beat 4 alone (measures 22–24), and a forceful half-measure fill using a 16th-eighth combination (measure 25). Here is the sticking that he most likely used in that fill. Watch for the same-hand flam accent on beat 4.

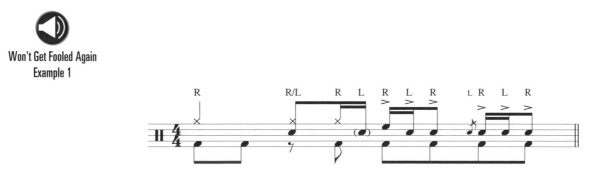

Won't Get Fooled Again
Example 1

First Verse

Moon continues the groove motif from the intro into the verse. From measure 32 to 33, he plays his signature continuous bass drum eighths, switching from single- to double-bass. A colorful fill in measure 33 garners our attention, as Moon's hands travel around the kit: middle tom, crash, snare, and floor tom.

First Chorus

Consecutive snare 16ths (with a couple of ghosted notes dropped in) lead us into what begins as a relatively reserved chorus on drums. Moon keeps it fresh by varying the bass drum from one measure to the next and employing four on the snare in measure 45. Starting in measure 48 when he phrases with the vocals, "pick up my guitar and play," Moon ratchets up the intensity and keeps it there through the rest of the chorus.

The four-bar phrase from measures 48–51 is turned into an exercise. The original passage is separated here between right hand and fills (both hands), kick (right foot) and snare (left hand), and then put back together again (all limbs). Notice that there is some overlap between fills and kick and snare.

Won't Get Fooled Again
Example 2

End of First Chorus/First Interlude

Towards the tail end of the chorus (measures 53–55) and the eight-bar instrumental interlude connecting the chorus to the next verse (measures 57–64), Moon seizes the moment and draws from his toolbox. He accents 16ths in measures 53 and 54, propels into the stop at measure 55 with a trademark four-stroke ruff on the 4 +, uses simultaneous double-kick to support off-beat crashes (measure 58), and crashes in two-measure phrases along with Townsend power chords like a big band drummer on 1 in the first measure and the 1 + of the second (measures 57–60). He also ventures out on his own with crashes on beat 2 in measure 57 and 59, and the 2 + in measure 58.

In the following three-part exercise, the concepts of accenting, combining 16th-notes with sextuplets, and phrasing using a 3:2 polyrhythm are represented on one surface and then shown similarly to how Moon plays—spread over a number of sound sources.

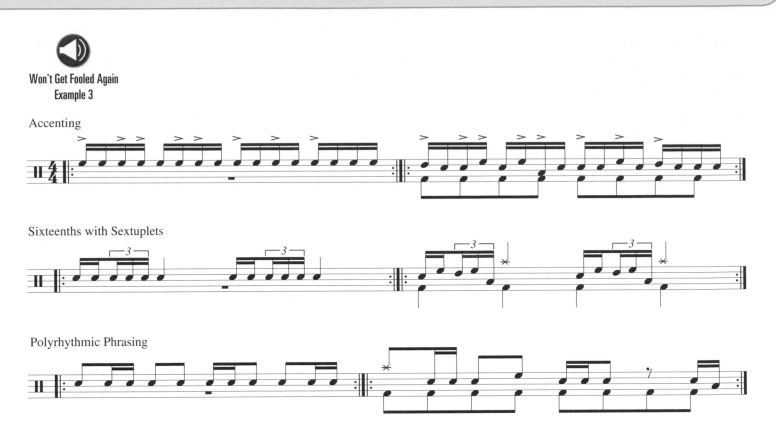

Second Verse

Moon plays another 3:2 fill (measure 72)—combining a five-stroke with a seven-stroke roll (and leftover single stroke)—and sprinkles ghosted notes throughout the section. Instead of consecutive 16ths, this time Moon leads into the next chorus by using two sets of power flam-flam tap combinations (each three eighths long) over simultaneous double-bass eighths (measure 80).

Second Chorus

He plays a busier second chorus, increasing the number of short fills: 16th bursts, four-stroke ruffs, and flat flams (in measures 94 and 95). Instead of stopping two bars after the word "pray," as he did previously, Moon drives all the way through the phrase, "we don't get fooled again." He plays another variation of the 3:2 polyrhythmic fill in measure 95.

Second Interlude

Moon plays pronounced off-beat crashes in measure 97 and then, starting in measure 100, he again lays down a sparse but powerful groove, building tension over an extended instrumental section into the bridge. Moon accentuates part of a guitar lick by adding simultaneous double-bass to beats 3, 3 +, and 4 (from measures 103–113). He repeats the idea of using straight 16ths mostly on the snare (measure 115) as a transitional device.

Bridge

The bridge features a sextuplet fill (measure 117) two beats long, as Moon again takes advantage of space between vocal phrases. The lick flows between high tom and snare. The following exercise shows two possible ways to stick the fill.

Won't Get Fooled Again
Example 4

Third Interlude/Guitar Solo/Retro

After one measure of overlapping explosiveness (measure 124), Moon simplifies, using mostly simultaneous double-bass, power flams on the snare, and crashes through a good portion of the guitar solo. He ramps up momentum from measures 139–148 until the retro (reintroduction) where, just like the beginning of the song, he supports Townsend's guitar. By allowing the chords (and cymbals) to ring out, Moon primes the pump for rest of the song.

Third Verse/Third Chorus

Moon is understated throughout the next verse and chorus; in fact, you can see how he leaves more space in measure 183 after the word "pray" than in the previous two choruses. He plays yet another inspired fill under the phrase "we don't get fooled again," overlapping syncopated power flams on the snare with simultaneous double-kick. Notice how he starts the fill on the 4 + of measure 185, accentuating the word "we"—something he didn't do in the other choruses. Coming out of this section, Moon continues playing off-beat crashes and two-beat 16th bursts.

Fourth Interlude

The Who improvise as a group—reflecting what they often did live—and Moon drums up a rhythmic idea in measures 191–192, which Townsend responds to starting in measure 201. Listen to how Moon adds excitement with simultaneous double-bass, four-stroke ruffs, and power flams. The 16th-note groupings grow longer and longer until, at measure 216, Moon plays consecutive 16ths all the way through the end of the jam at measure 222. His passion for surf drumming is on full display.

Beginning in measure 199, and a number of successive measures, Moon plays a four-stroke ruff combination of both kicks, snare, floor tom, both kicks/middle tom (or other sound source) located on the 2 +. The following exercise will help you get a hang of this thunderous lick. The first measure gets your feet moving with double-bass eighth notes, while the second measure includes the actual lick from measure 199.

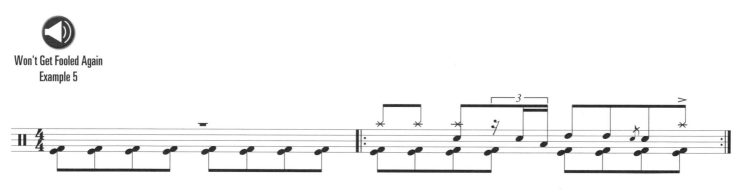

Won't Get Fooled Again
Example 5

Try It

Using *Playback+* from the accompanying audio, loop the seven-bar phrase from 216–222 and improvise 16ths over eighth-note bass drum. Try to use a number of sound sources: crash, snare, high tom, middle tom, snare, and floor tom. Besides making split-second decisions on what to play next, the greater challenge might be to keep your intensity level up through the entire passage, as Moon always does.

Drum Solo

After a lengthy synth interlude (measures 223–247), Moon plays what has become one of the most recognizable drum solos in the history of pop music. Let's take a look at what makes these three phrases over seven bars so appealing.

The synth part that precedes the first drum phrase is just random enough, while still clearly delineating downbeats, that the listener craves something recognizable amidst the buildup of tension. The 6/4 bar (measure 246) is a mirage and plants a seed of doubt that isn't completely resolved until a Daltrey scream that anticipates the downbeat of the outro. It's possible that Moon himself may have been confused, and that's why he started his first phrase on beat 3 of measure 254!

Whether on purpose or by accident, Moon's entrance in the middle of measure 254 is striking and unusual. It sets up a call-and-response between synth and drums. Moon also ends each phrase in obvious ways—floor tom and bass drum flat flams in the first two phrases—which gives the listener the necessary goal posts.

Each phrase is longer than the next, which creates momentum all the way through the solo. Strategically placed near the end, the solo could easily be thought of as the climax of the entire tune.

The Big Picture

Though "Won't Get Fooled Again" is perfect for copying drum licks, it's Moon's ability to shape the energy level from beginning to end that's most stunning. He does this by using dynamics (from measure to measure, phrase to phrase, and section to section), sound source choices, rhythmic design, and space. He uses the outro as a denouement, bringing in some of the thematic material that he established earlier, such as crashes on beat 4 and four-stroke ruffs, but mostly plays sparsely. This helps bring the song to a satisfying close.

WON'T GET FOOLED AGAIN

Words and Music by Peter Townshend

Won't Get Fooled Again
Full Song

Intro
Moderately fast ♩ = 135

*Sloshy hi-hat throughout song

Verse

fight - ing in the streets ___ with our chil - dren at our feet, ___

___ and the mor - als that they wor - ship will be gone. ___

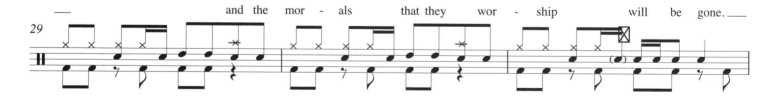

___ And the men who spurred us on ___

___ sit in judge - ment of all wrong; ___ they de -

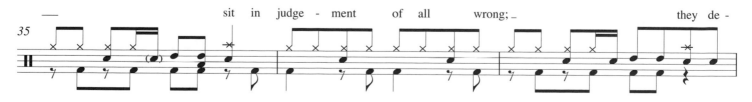

cide,   and   the shot   gun   sings   the song. ___

Chorus

I'll   tip   my   hat   to the   new   con - sti - tu - tion,

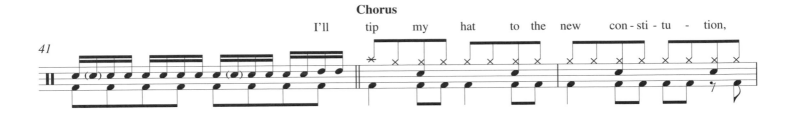

take   a   bow ___   for the   new   rev - o - lu   -   tion.   Smile and   grin ___   at the

change   all   a - round.   Pick up my gui - tar   and   play ___

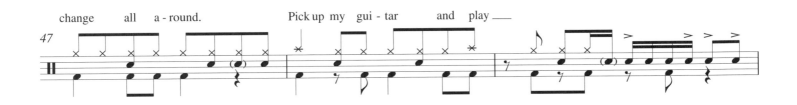

just   like   yes - ter - day. ___   Then I'll   get on   my   knees   and

pray   we

Interlude

don't   get fooled ___   a - gain.

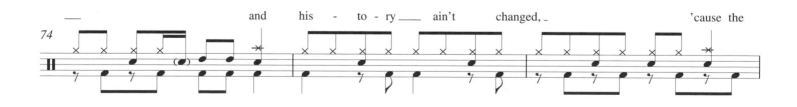

Chorus

I'll tip my hat to the new con-sti-tu-tion, take a bow for the new rev-o-lu-tion. Smile and grin at the change all a-round. Pick up my gui-tar and play just like yes-ter-day. Then I'll get on my knees and

pray we

Interlude

don't get fooled a-gain. No, no!

I'll

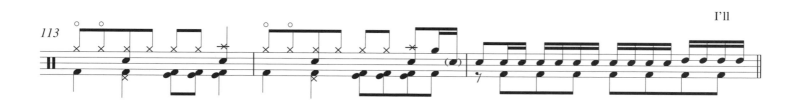

Bridge

move my - self and my fam-'ly a - side, ____ if we hap-pen to be

left half __ a - live. _____ I'll get all my pa - pers and smile __ at the sky. Oh, I

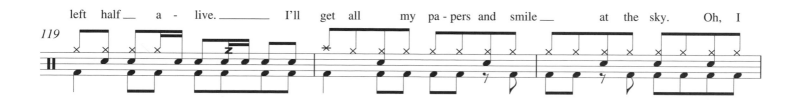

know that the hyp-no-tized nev-er lie.

Interlude

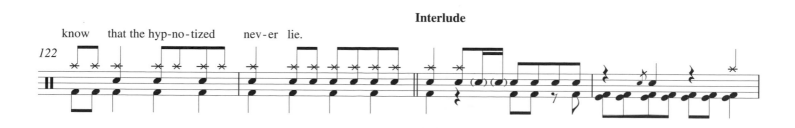

Do   ya?

Guitar Solo

Retro

Yeah! 3. There's

Verse

noth - ing   in   the   street   looks   an - y   dif - fer - ent   to   me,

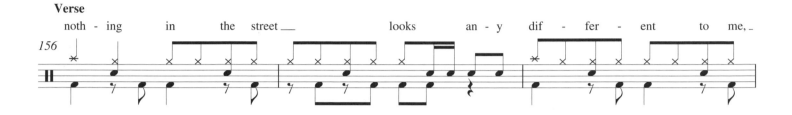

    and   the   slo - gans   are re - placed   by   the   by.

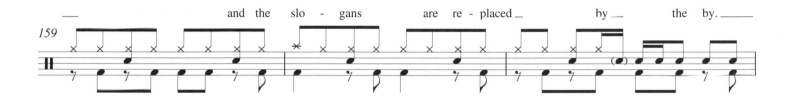

    And   the   part - ing   on   the left

    is   now   part - ing   on   the   right,   and   the

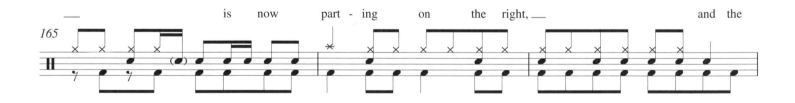

beards   have   all   grown   long - er   o - ver - night.

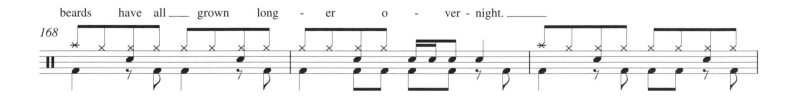

Chorus

I'll   tip   my   hat   to   the   new   con - sti - tu - tion,

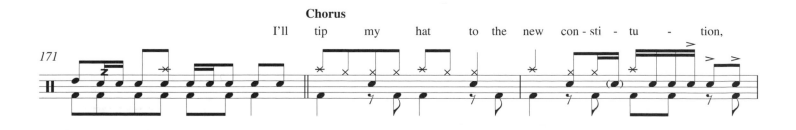

take a bow___ for the new rev - o - lu - tion. Smile and grin___ at the

174

change all a - round. Pick up my gui - tar and play___

177

just like yes - ter - day.___ Then I'll get on my knees and

180

pray we

183

don't get fooled___ a - gain.___ Don't get fooled a - gain.___

186

Interlude

___ No, no!

189

192

Interlude

Drum Solo

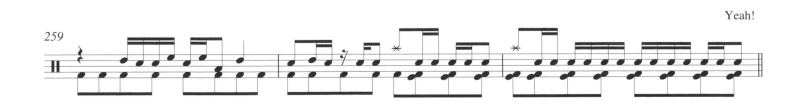

Outro

Meet   the   new   ___   boss.   Same   as   the   old   boss.

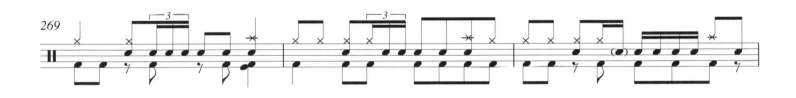

Rubato

Bargain
From *Who's Next*, 1971

"Everything about the song reeks of prime Who, including the powerhouse performance by Moon. But it's not all manic bashing. At times, he shows off his range by pulling in, ever so slightly, and allowing the song room to breathe." [Ultimateclassicrock.com]

Another track off the seminal album *Who's Next*, "Bargain" is a case study of a rock group in top form. Townsend's layered guitar, John Entwhistle's frenetic bass lines, Daltrey's powerful vocals, and Moon's elegant drumming are all on full display. Moon phrases with and around the vocal melody, uses articulations including accents and ghosted notes, and plays rudiments including ruffs and flams.

Intro

A floaty guitar melody over acoustic guitar strumming (don't forget the rockin' tambourine!) takes place in the first six bars, momentarily taking the listener to a fantasy soundscape. Moon jolts us into reality with a meandering two-bar fill starting on beat 3 of measure 7. Though improvised in the heat of the moment, this fiery opening gives us a window into how his influences affect his drum parts. Starting with a half-note rest may have been a happy accident—maybe he wasn't ready to come in—but is more likely a nod to jazz drummers (Philly Joe Jones was one of Moon's favorites), who often start phrases before or after the downbeat. You can simulate this by utilizing the following four-bar structure. During the two-beat pause, make sure to still keep time by tapping the heel of your left foot or nodding your head.

Bargain
Example 1

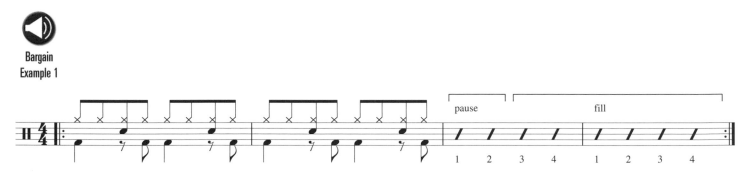

Moon is often characterized as a heavy-hitter. This is, of course, based in truth; his aggression frequently took him to the top of the dynamic spectrum. However, a closer look reveals Moon's use of subtle devises, such as the drag leading into beat 3 of the opening fill.

Some 16th-note accents reinforced by bass drum hits, a technique employed by big band drummers such as Buddy Rich, complete most of the rest of the fill. To give you a better handle on this, the following accent pattern is gleaned from Moon's phrase but pared down to one surface to give you the freedom to orchestrate the accents your own way. The bass drum notes below the accents are surrounded by parentheses, giving you the choice to play these or not.

Bargain
Example 2

As mentioned about the two previous tunes ("Pinball Wizard" and "Won't Get Fooled Again"), Moon had obvious leanings towards the sound of the four-stroke ruff, in which he played around the kit in numerous ways. In "Bargain," this rudiment consistently starts on the 3 + and finishes on 4. The following exercise takes this one step further by adding ruffs on the 1 +. You'll also observe continuous bass drum eighth notes and ruffs orchestrated around the toms.

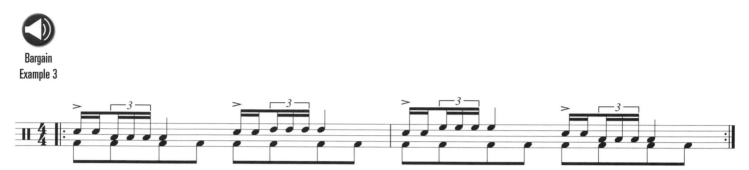

Bargain
Example 3

First Verse

Moon had the ability to take in all of the rhythmic and melodic information coming at him and respond in the moment. In the case of the first verse of "Bargain," observe how the bass drum pattern follows the rhythm of the melody and the syllables in the lyrics.

Try It
Learn to sing the first verse—even if you're not such a great vocalist. Next, sing while playing along with the full drum transcription of the first verse. Repeat the process, but this time, create your own drum groove to accompany your vocals.

To keep the music from getting dull, Moon liked to vary his groove patterns. The first verse is a great example of this; in fact, no two measures are alike. The following exercise is constructed from beats found in the first verse. To encourage a Moon mindset, two blank measures are included to give you a chance to create your own patterns. Make sure your beats are different in some way from each of the others.

Bargain
Example 4

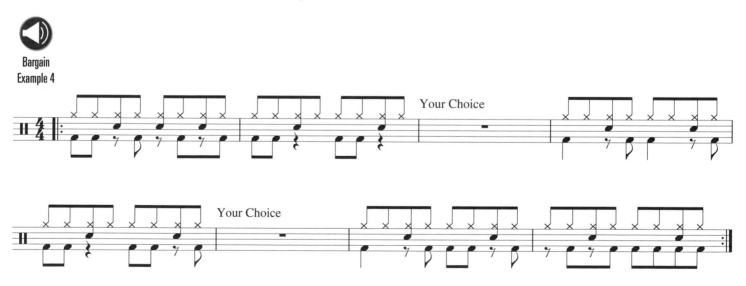

First Chorus

An almost completely symmetrical eighth-note fill (measure 24) spotlights the phrase "I'd call that a bargain" and melds perfectly with the bass line. From measures 25–27, Moon uses restraint by playing only downbeat crashes in the first three measures, following with a bombastic three measures of lead drums over big guitar/bass chords.

Here are the hands-only drum parts from measures 28–30 (first chorus) and 54–56 (second chorus), with each phrase condensed down to one surface. Follow the sticking recommendations and add bass drum when you're ready. Finally, include the sound source variations from the full transcription.

**Bargain
Example 5**

First Interlude

Clear away the crashes, four-stroke ruffs, and extraneous 16ths (adding a few hi-hats and one snare), and you arrive at a simplification of the interlude groove. Notice how the first/third and second/fourth measures of this section use similar bass drum patterns. Moon may have chosen these beats to balance the bass and guitar rhythms.

**Bargain
Example 6**

Third Interlude

Longer than previous sections, the third interlude is split between six bars without synth (measures 79–84) and 16 bars with synth (measures 85–100). Notice how Moon gradually builds intensity from the beginning to the end of this interlude by adding bass drum eighth notes, four-stroke ruffs, off-beat crashes, and groupings of 16ths. The accented 16ths in measure 92 stand out and are somewhat reminiscent of Gene Krupa's "Sing, Sing, Sing."

The following exercise uses the accenting pattern from measure 92 along with others found throughout "Bargain." Though shown on one surface, feel free to place the accented notes on other parts of the drum kit and to add Moon's distinctive bass drum eighths.

Bargain
Example 7

Outro

After another song cycle (verse, chorus, and interlude), an outro begins at measure 135, and Moon again delays his entrance two beats (measure 142). The pattern in measure 143 sounds like Moon is using double-bass as part of sextuplet combinations, but he's actually using his floor tom. Suggested sticking is included here for measures 143–149.

Bargain
Example 8

To finish out the tune, Moon plays a flow of sextuplets between crash and ghosted snare starting in measure 150, breaks into a free-wheeling, mostly 16th-note groove from measure 153–158, plays repeated four-stroke ruffs between bass drum/middle tom, snare, and crash (measure 159), and then blasts mostly continuous sextuplets with his hands (measure 161–172).

The Big Picture

As mentioned in the introduction of this book, Moon was a risk-taker on and off the stage. Even in the freewheeling '60s and '70s, when it was common for drummers to play extended solos, long fills, and varied patterns, he was extremely free in his approach—so free that listeners often mistake his playing as haphazard and unrestrained. This is just not the case. In fact, "Bargain" demonstrates his innate ability to walk a thin line between taking chances and following a structure.

As a youngster, Moon spent countless hours listening to, absorbing, and miming his favorites. When he got behind the drum kit, he had an uncanny ability to draw from these influences. Though he had to stay within parameters dictated to him through Townsend and Johns, Moon demonstrates his early influences throughout "Bargain."

If you want to capture his unique brand of musicianship, you need to both harness Moon's controlled chaos and listen to (and copy) his favorites. The "Must Hear" and "Must See" chapters at the end of the book will get you off to a good start.

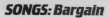

BARGAIN
Words and Music by Peter Townshend

Chorus

I'd call that a bar - gain, the best I ev - er

had. The

best I ev - er had. _____

Interlude

Verse

2. I'd glad - ly lose ___ me to find _

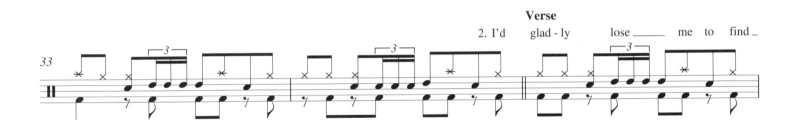

___ you, 'n' glad - ly give up all ___ I got. ___ To

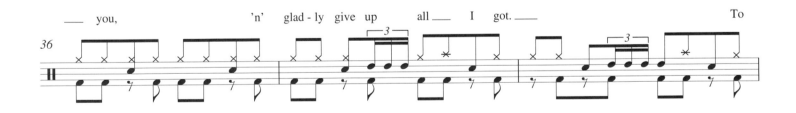

catch you, I'm gon - na run ___ 'n' nev - er stop. ___

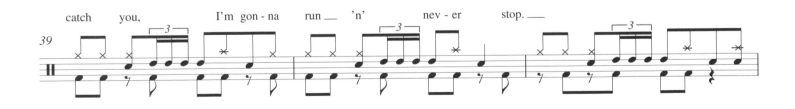

I'll pay an - y price ___ just to win you, sur -

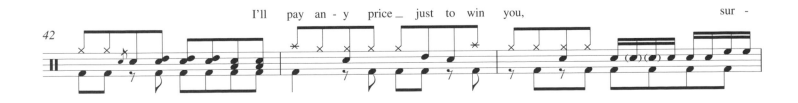

ren - der my good _ life for bad. ___ To find you, I'm gon - na

drown an un - sung man. ___ I call that a

Chorus

bar - gain, the best I ev - er had.

The

Interlude

best I ev - er had. _____

Bridge
Half-time feel

I sit look - in' 'round, ___ I look at my face _

Verse

3. I'd glad ly lose ____ me to find ____ you,

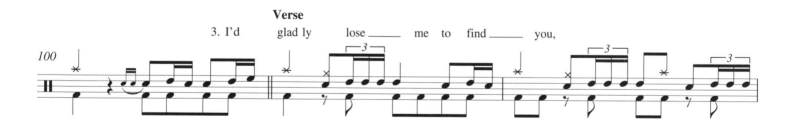

glad - ly give up all ____ I got. ____ To catch you, I'm gon - na

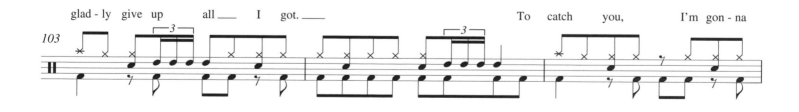

run ____ and nev - er stop. I'll

pay an - y price _ just to win _____ you, sur - ren - der my good life for

bad. To find you, I'm gon - na drown _ an un - sung man. _

Chorus
I call that a bar - gain, the

best I ev - er had.

The best I ev - er had. __

Interlude

130

132

Outro

134

142

144

146

148

149

150

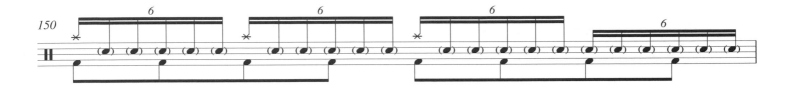

151

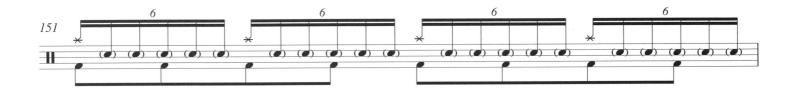

152

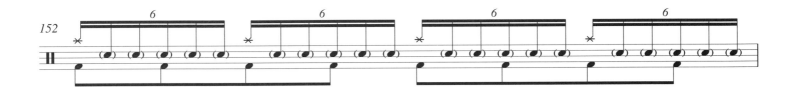

153

155

157

Half-time feel

Love, Reign o'er Me
From *Quadrophenia*, 1973

"When I first played with the Who, we did *Quadrophenia*. There were certain things that had to be in there, certain fills that had to be exactly the same because they are so *Quadrophenia*, if you know what I mean. They are memorable fills. There aren't memorable parts, though, because everything Keith played kept changing." [Zac Starkey, Modern Drummer]

"…You know, there's so many drummers that can go through the routine, but they don't add color anywhere…I like painting, adding color and effects, and shocking people." [Keith Moon]

For whatever reason, Moon got a reputation for not being able to handle time signatures outside of 4/4. You would never guess that from listening to "Love, Reign o'er Me." Not only does he play groove patterns and fills with ease (giving us a whole new batch of Moon-isms), but he also breaks away from the conventional approach by playing a number of cymbals swells/rolls over long swaths of music, providing texture and a unique backdrop for the vocal melody.

Intro/First Verse

After 56 seconds of the sound of rain, piano noodling, and timpani rolls by Moon (plus a nice loud China cymbal hit), we're almost relieved when the piano begins to establish time in 6. Moon plays eighth-notes crash crescendos every other measure (4–19)—an obvious nod to rain falling—all the way to an exciting, perfectly executed fill in measure 20. The fill involves bass drum eighths, a melody originating on the snare and moving to middle tom and floor tom, and a flam tap on 5. Moon also starts the fill one eighth note (two 16ths here) before the downbeat of measure 20, giving it a jazzy vibe.

Try It
To attain the smoothest possible cymbal swell/roll (and to create a mallet effect), use the shoulder of the stick against the edge of the cymbal.

First Chorus

Moon varies the groove in 6/8 the same way we've seen him do in 4/4: just about every measure is slightly different than the one that precedes it. From what we know about his personality, it's likely that these decisions were made in the moment. To simulate this, his tendencies in 6/8 are shown in 3/8 rhythmic seeds. Your job is to mix and match by combining any element from the first group with any element from the second group.

Love, Reign o'er Me
    Example 1

Throughout each of the three choruses, Moon adds a feeling of three-dimensionality by accenting crash cymbal hits in one or more of the six eighth-note positions. In the following exercise, this concept is applied to one of Moon's patterns in the chorus.

Love, Reign o'er Me
Example 2

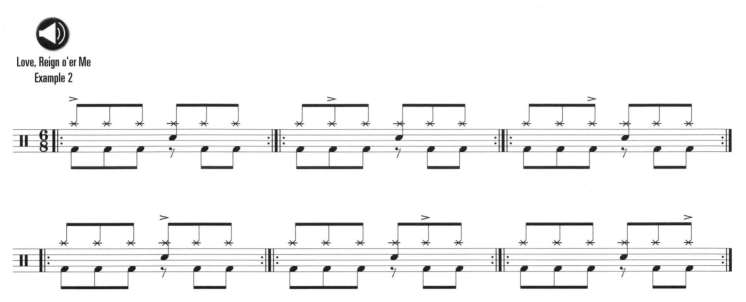

As the first chorus ends, notice the subtleties: a five-stroke roll (using buzz strokes) on beat 2 through 3 in measure 36, and all of the space that he leaves from measure 37–40, which provides a smooth transition into the second verse.

Second Chorus

Moon picks up the intensity in this section by increasing rhythmic density. The added notes are mostly four- or five-note groupings involving four-stroke ruffs on beats 2 and 5 and single-stroke fives (five-stroke roll using singles) on beats 1 and 4.

In measures 66 and 67, Moon pounds out bass drum eighths but implies a 3-over-2 polyrhythm by accenting the crash/snare on 1 and 5 and snare on 3. In the following exercise, the bass drum and first three sextuplets of each four-stroke ruff are stripped away to reveal the core of what Moon is playing with his hands in the two-bar phrase. The actual phrase is shown directly underneath the stripped-down version.

Love, Reign o'er Me
Example 3

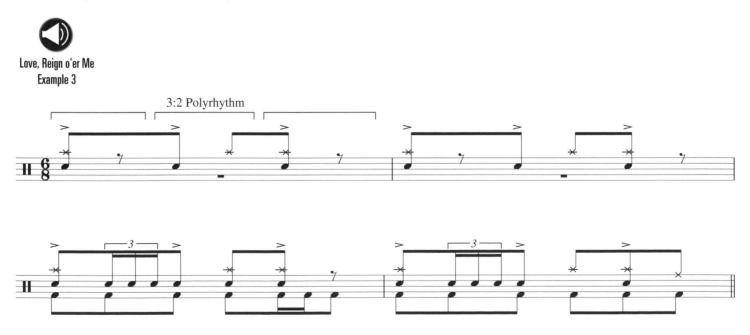

Moon plays a skeletal four-bar phrase starting in measure 73. This affects a change to a low dynamic, while an eighth-note pulse on the bass drum continues seamlessly into the bridge.

Guitar Solo

Townsend plays a 16-bar guitar solo over the verse harmony, and Moon sticks with his plan: He again plays cymbal swells every other measure. Different than the first two verses (when Moon mixes eighth and 16th-note rolls), in the guitar solo, he plays all 16th-note cymbal rolls.

While cymbal rolls can be played as an ambiguous, out-of-time effect, Moon always played precise rolls based on the available rhythmic pulsations. In "Love, Reign o'er Me," he plays either eighths or 16ths as single strokes (shown in the example as A and B), but many other choices are possible. Included here is a sampling of the available options.

    A. Eighth notes (singles)

    B. 16ths (singles)

    C. 16ths (doubles)

    D. Sextuplets (singles)

    E. Sextuplets (doubles)

Love, Reign o'er Me
Example 4

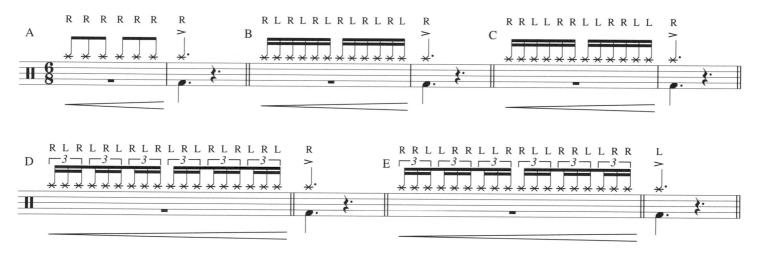

NOTE: When playing double strokes on cymbals, you will need to make contact with the tip of the stick against any part of the top portion, though it's most common to play an inch or two from the edge.

Try It
Using *Playback+* from the accompanying audio, loop measures 117–132. Try the cymbal swell options covered in the "Love Reign o'er Me," Example 4.

Big Ending

After a beat-and-a-half cymbal roll to begin measure 157 (5:02), Moon plays out of time, indistinguishable 16ths with his hands around the kit along with bass drum eighths. At measure 169, the time shifts into a sextuplet-based feel as Moon plays downbeat crashes along with power chords.

Let's face it; recorded pop music doesn't normally include 22-measure extended finales. The Who made a habit of breaking through barriers like this. Of course, it may have helped to have such a free-spirited percussionist on their team.

The Big Picture

Moon adds color and texture throughout "Love, Reign o'er Me," allowing his creativity to drive his choices. Much of this has already been detailed in the section-by-section analysis of the song.

As drummers, we have an awe-inspiring number of sound source options at our disposal. (Moon had many more than the average drummer.) It can be difficult to know what object to strike at what time. Here are a few tips to help you make these decisions in your band.

- **Short sounds or long sounds**: Closed hi-hit, snare, and bass drum have fairly short durations; toms normally ring out (unless muted) for a fairly long time, and cymbals have an incredibly long sustain unless choked. Think about how the sustain of different parts of your drum set matches or contrasts the other instruments in the band.

- **Frequencies**: Drum set components run the gamut from high to low frequencies. It's important to support (and not mask) the other instruments and vocals. Moon does a great job of varying frequencies with his hands while often supporting with lows from his bass drum(s).

- **Simplicity or complexity**: Townsend often commented about having to hold down the fort while Moon and Entwistle were able to take chances. There is some truth behind this, but there are also plenty of instances in Who music when drums and/or bass play it safe. The important thing is to find the right balance to best serve the music.

Love, Reign o'er Me
Full Song

LOVE, REIGN O'ER ME

Words and Music by Peter Townshend

Chorus

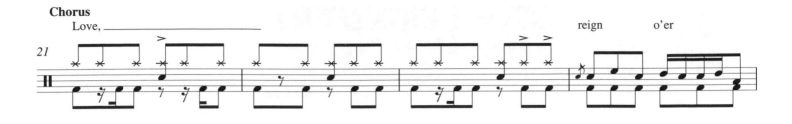

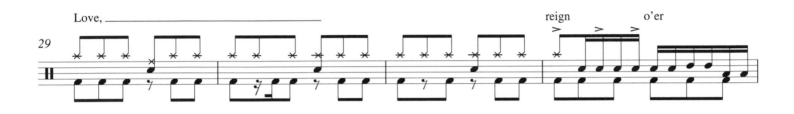

Verse

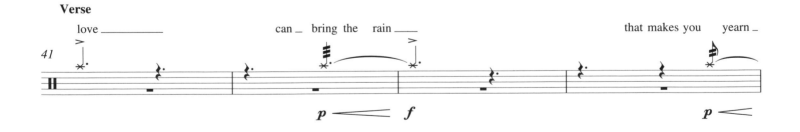

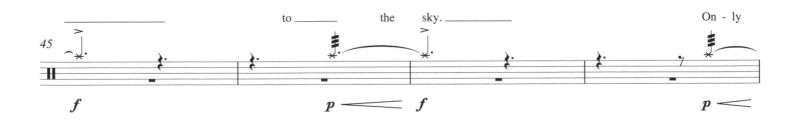

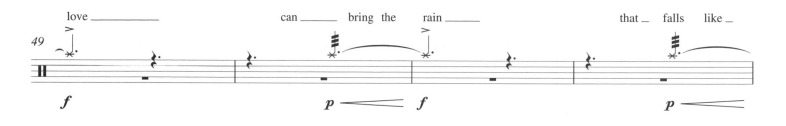

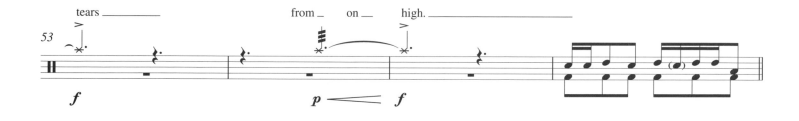

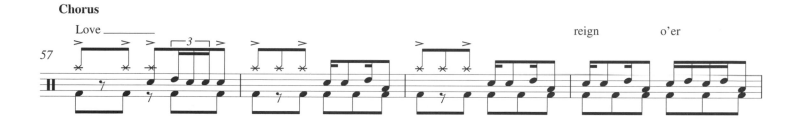

Chorus

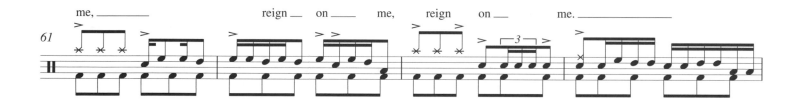

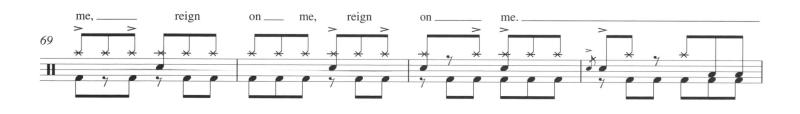

Bridge

On the　dry and dust-y road,　　　the nights　we　spent a-part　a - lone,

I　need＿　to　get back home　　to　cool＿＿＿　cool＿＿＿　rain.＿＿＿＿＿

I can't　sleep＿ and　I　lay and I think,

the night is　hot　and black as　ink,　　　woo, uh,＿ God I＿　need a　drink＿　　　of

cool＿＿＿　cool＿　　rain.＿＿＿＿＿＿＿＿＿

Guitar Solo

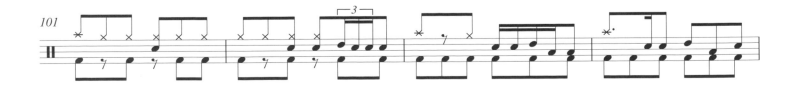

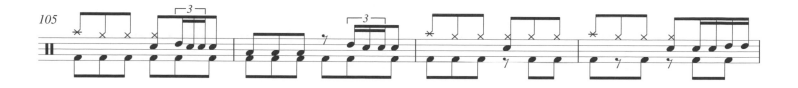

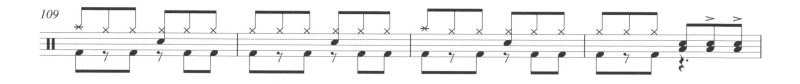

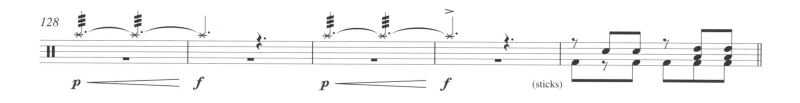

Chorus

Love, _____ reign o'er

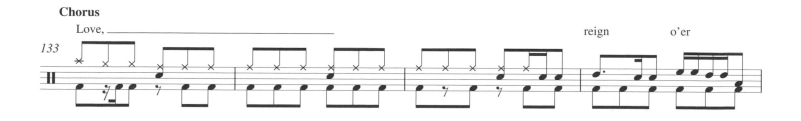

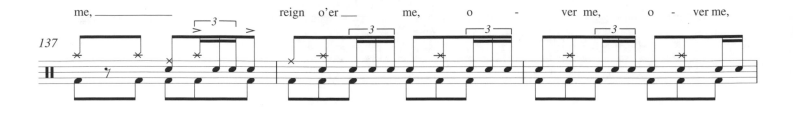

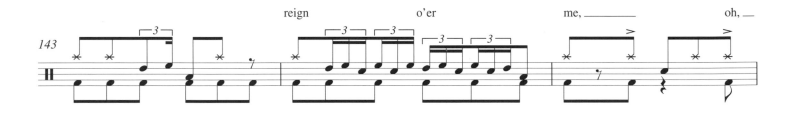

Outro
Free time

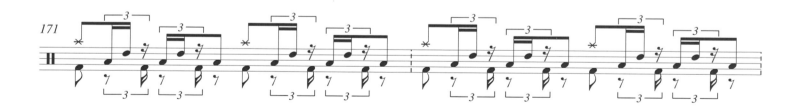

Who Are You
From *Who Are You*, 1978

"While most drummers would use a more consistent pattern, Moon changes his from measure to measure. Surprise and spontaneity were strong characteristics of his drumming." [*Drum! Magazine Online* 2013]

When Moon recorded his drum parts to "Who Are You," he was not in the best mental or physical state. Before going in to record the album, his drumming chops had deteriorated, and his confidence had vanished because of lack of rehearsal, touring, and recording. A testament to his passion for being in the Who, Moon was still able to pull off one of his all-time best performances.

His drumming on "Who Are You" is somewhat reflective of late '70s rock—clarity and simplicity began to become fashionable—but nevertheless, Moon put his stamp on the music with dynamics, texture, creativity, and phrasing.

First Chorus

After a six-measure half-time intro with electronic hand claps over programmed synth, syncopated bass, and bluesy guitar riffing, the feel in the chorus changes to "regular time." In other words, the pulse of the chorus is double the tempo of the intro. Moon does something that no drummer would ever think to do; he plays a hi-hat march with sloshy accents—a counter to Daltrey's vocal melody.

NOTE: Accented notes are executed by the shoulder (shank) of the stick striking the edge of the hi-hat, while the tip of the stick bounces off the top of the hi-hat.

Moon plays the hi-hat in the 16-bar first chorus (in very much the same way as he does the fourth chorus starting in measure 124) in a spontaneous manner. Moon is most likely improvising off a counter-melody heard in his head. What comes out is a slew of 16ths (with some eighths) and a number of accents. A deeper analysis reveals these tendencies.
- Beats 1 and 3 are accented in every measure.
- The 1 *a* is frequently accented.
- Moon likes to accent consecutive 16ths. Here, he plays five or six successive accents starting on the 2 *a* or 3 and going all the way to beat 4.
- When Moon leaves space between 16ths—except for the dotted eighth note to 16th rhythm on beat 2 of measure 15—he normally combines one eighth with two 16ths.
- The last measure (28) is an outlier used to transition into the first verse.

In the following exercise, space (notated as rests) is infused into the 16-bar first chorus. Keeping Moon's tendencies in mind, your job is to fill in those empty spaces.

Who Are You
Example 1

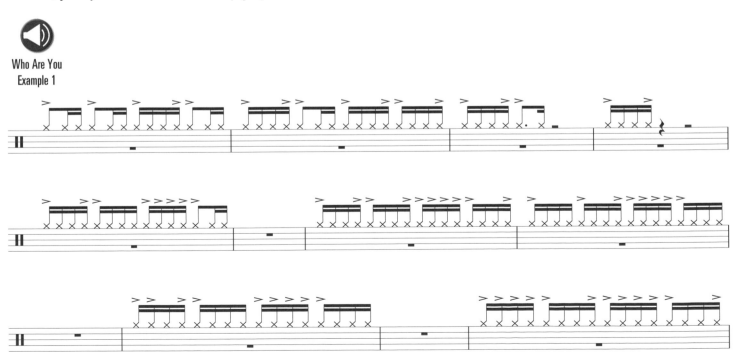

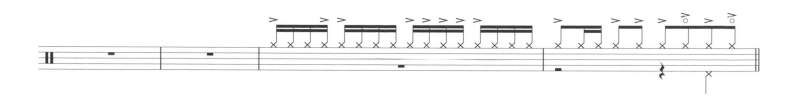

First Verse

The Who slip back into a half-time feel, and Moon plays a funky beat (measures 29–44) using a formula that goes along with the vocal melody: three bars of time + one bar of fill. The following exercise examines measures 29–36. The hi-hat and crash (right hand and left foot) are separated from the kick and snare (left hand and right foot), showing the interweaving, three-dimensionality of the groove. The fills are left out to better help you focus on time playing. Learn each part separately and then put them back together. NOTE: On the accompanying audio, the click sounds in half time to simulate the half-time feel.

Who Are You
Example 2

The Who went into the studio in July of 1978 with the intention of shooting promotional footage in support of the newly released single, "Who Are You." They were going to mime along with the song but ended up playing so well to the original master that their performance was recorded and eventually used in the film, *The Kids Are Alright*.

Moon's re-recorded playing demonstrates his penchant for varying his patterns. For instance, the groove that he plays in the first verse sounds more like New Orleans/Caribbean funk than a more straightforward approach in the single edit version. When you watch/listen to the footage, you can actually witness the intense eye contact that Moon makes with Townsend and Entwistle while laying down the track. Included here is a transcription taken from the first verse of the version from *The Kids Are Alright*. Notice how he hits two crashes (right-side and left-side) at the same time on beat 3 (replacing the typical snare backbeat and turning the beat upside down), with only an eighth-note space to make the maneuver.

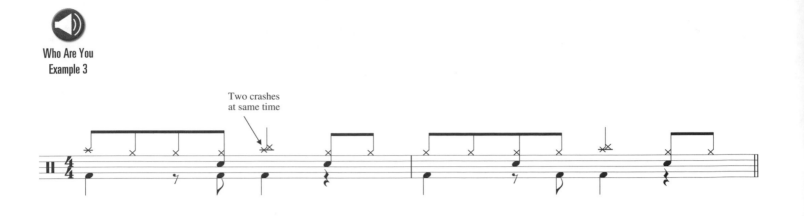

Who Are You
Example 3

Two crashes
at same time

Try It
Using *Playback+* from the accompanying audio, loop measures 29–44. Using ideas from both of Moon's performances, create your own version. Make it as spontaneous as possible.

Second Chorus/Second Verse/Third Chorus

In the second chorus, Moon launches into a driving, hyperactive disco beat. Notice how he keeps us on the edge of our seats by varying his bass drum pattern and playing a couple of short 16th-note fills on the snare.

Moon ups the ante in the second verse by crashing into the ride in the first two measures, playing a Chinese cymbal/snare hit on beat 3 in measure 66, and playing rhythmically dense two-beat fills—combinations of eighths and 16ths—at the end of each four-bar phrase. He keeps his foot on the accelerator going into the third chorus, staying on the ride cymbal (and interjecting ride crashes in key spots), playing funky hits on the 2 *e* and 4 *e* in measure 87, and creating three one-measure long 16th-oriented fills in measures 84, 88, and 92.

Interlude

A breakdown/interlude begins at measure 93, giving the listener a short respite with synth, lead acoustic guitar, and no drums. When Moon, Townsend (on electric guitar), and Entwistle enter on beat 3 in measure 115, we're startled, but in a good way. Moon handles the eight-bar phrase from measures 115–122 with simplicity. He crashes along with band hits on beat 3, adding a big-band style set-up in measure 120. A Chinese cymbal on the downbeat of measure 123 showcases a refreshing, new sound in Moon's repertoire; he had only just begun to use this type of cymbal.

Bridge

An ethereal section of synth, bass, and a falsetto chant lasts from measures 123–154 and includes an overdub of Moon playing timpani. He again plays a sparse-but-melodic drum part, supporting the vocal chant, until a huge two-measure quarter-note triplet fill (along with bass and guitar) is unleashed in measure 145. Notice how Moon varies the flat flams by keeping his left hand on the high tom, while moving his right around the kit. An eight-bar instrumental phrase finishes off the section and leads us into the fourth chorus.

Fourth Chorus/Fifth Chorus

Moon plays this section similarly to the first chorus (hi-hat only) but additionally plays off a frenetic piano part. In the fifth chorus (full-on drum kit), Moon drives the groove with eighth notes on the bass drum. Starting in measure 186, he begins an onslaught of one-measure (or slightly less) fills chained together, like a fireworks finale, over Daltrey's aggressive howling.

The Big Picture

As mentioned previously, Moon played drums at a time when improvisation was more valued than the repetition and quantized accuracy so common today. Moon played with a sense of urgency that helped the Who become one of the great rock bands of all time. If you want to sound like him (and create a masterpiece such as "Who Are You"), you will have to keep the following in mind:

- Your groove doesn't have to be constructed in two- or four-bar chunks. In fact, it's all right to vary your beat from measure to measure. Listen to the other instruments or the vocal melody to instruct your playing.
- Fills can be of any length as long as they add to the flow of the music.
- Drums are not just a tool for accompaniment; Moon often used drums as a melodic instrument, such as during the breakdown/interlude of "Who Are You." Feel free to create melodies that stand alone, are supportive, and are counter to existing melodies.

WHO ARE YOU
Words and Music by Peter Townshend

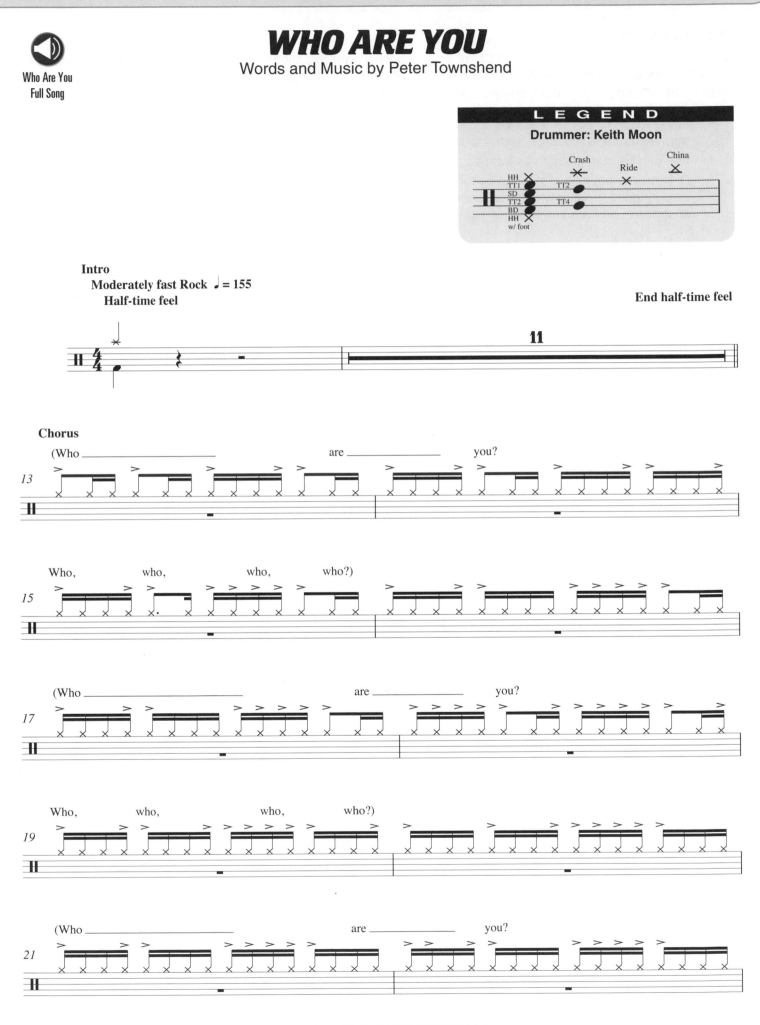

Who,   who,   who,   who?)

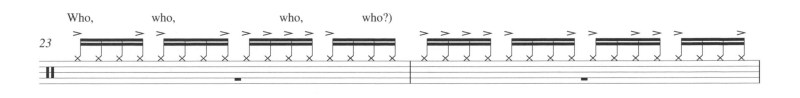

(Who _____ are _____ you?

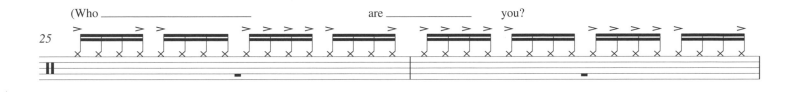

Who,   who,   who,   who?)

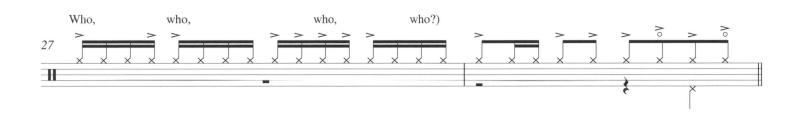

Verse
Half-time feel

1. I woke up in a So - ho door - way, a po - lice - man knew my

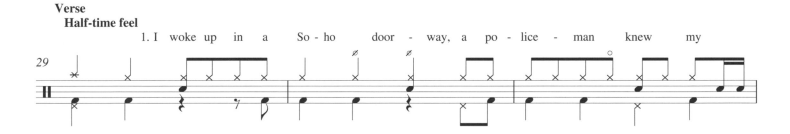

name.   He said,   "You can go sleep at home ___ to - night ___ if you can

get up and walk ___ a - way." _____   I stag-gered back to the un -

- der - ground, ___ and the breeze ___ blew back my hair.

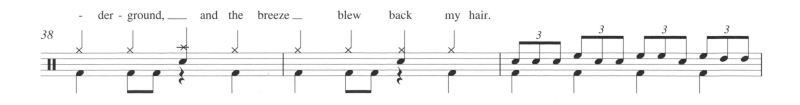

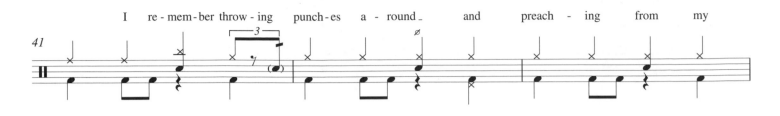

I re-mem-ber throw-ing punch-es a-round and preach-ing from my

41

Chorus
End half-time feel

chair.   Well, who are you?
                                          (Who _____ are _____ you?

44

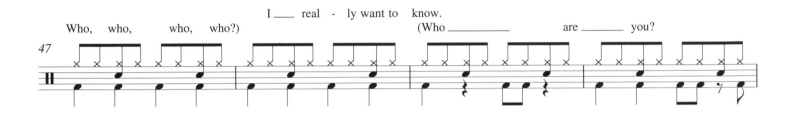

I ___ real - ly want to know.   (Who _____ are _____ you?
Who, who, who, who?)

47

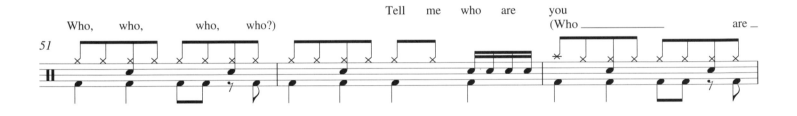

Tell me who are you
Who, who, who, who?)   (Who _____ are _

51

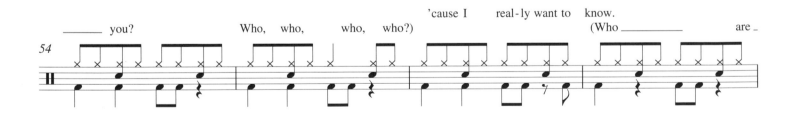

                                       'cause I real-ly want to know.
_____ you?   Who, who, who, who?)   (Who _____ are _

54

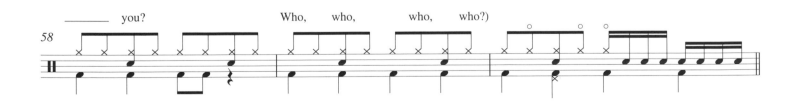

_____ you?   Who, who, who, who?)

58

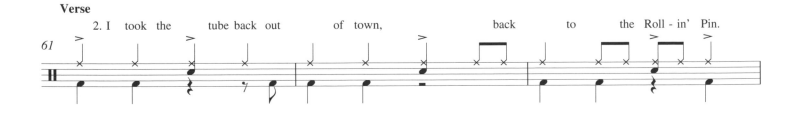

Verse

2. I took the tube back out of town,   back to the Roll - in' Pin.

61

I felt a lit - tle like a dy - ing clown with a

64

streak of Rin Tin Tin. I stretched back and I hic -

67

cupped, _____ and looked back on my bus - y day.

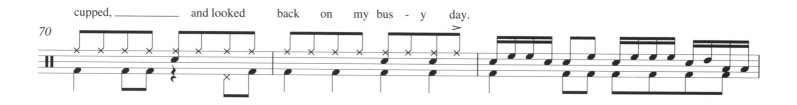

70

E - lev - en hours in the Tin Pan; God, there's got to be an - oth - er

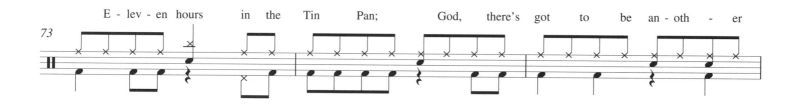

73

Chorus

way. Well, who are you?
(Who _____ are _____ you?

76

Oh, _____ who are you?
Who, who, who, who?) (Who _____ are _____ you?

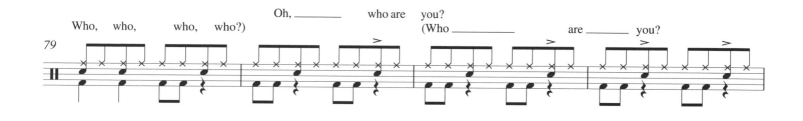

79

C' - mon, tell me who are you?
Who, who, who, who?) (Who _____ are _

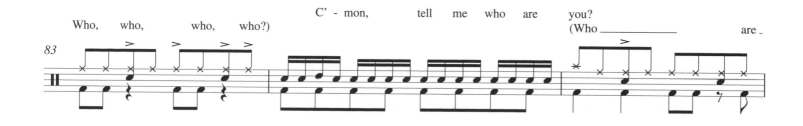

83

Interlude

21

Half-time feel

End half-time feel

Bridge

Do, da, — do, da, do, da, do, da, — do, da, do.

Do, da, — do, da, do, da, do, da, — do, da, do.

*Played w/ soft mallets, next 13 meas.

Chorus

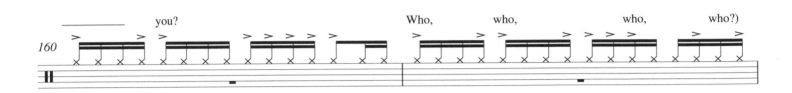

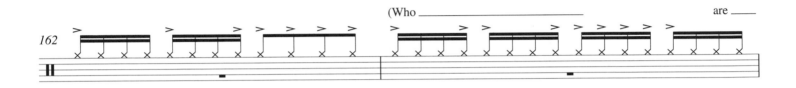

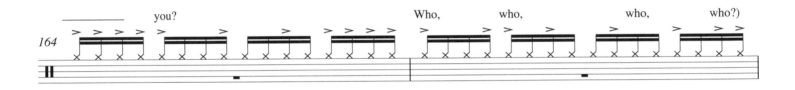

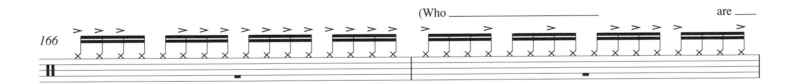

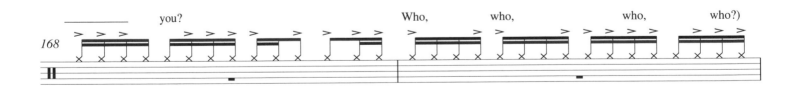

Outro Chorus

Who, who,   who,   who?)   Ah,   who   the   f*** are   you?
                                                              (Who _____   are _

173

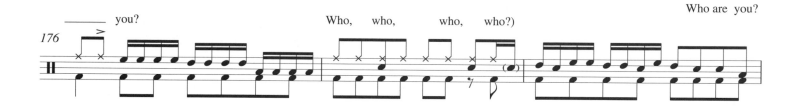

___ you?   Who,   who,   who,   who?)   Who are you?

176

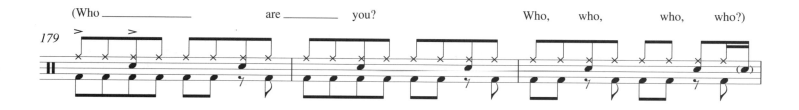

(Who _____   are _____ you?   Who,   who,   who,   who?)

179

Oh   tell   me   who   are   you?
                                          (Who _____   are _____ you?

182

                         I   real - ly   wan - na   know.
                                                        (Who?

Who?)

185

Oh, I   real - ly   wan - na   know.   Come on,   tell me who are
                        Who?

188

you?   You?   Ah!   You!
Ah!)

191

ESSENTIAL GROOVES

Moon's approach was so unique that there's a lot of confusion and misconceptions about his groove playing. Mike Portnoy, who did an incredible job emulating Moon in his Amazing Journey project, said the following: "Keith played like a total hurricane... He didn't ever play a solid backbeat or groove. He was a whirlwind of tom fills and cymbal swells, and his kick drums were always pulsating. Rather than laying down a solid groove and foundation, he was constantly playing circles around it." While some of Portnoy's comments here are right on the money, others could be described as overgeneralizations. This chapter provides a balanced look into some of Moon's iconic beats.

Moon played so many signature grooves over the course of his short but illustrious career that it's hard to narrow it down to a short list. Nevertheless, here are seven distinct examples representing 1965 to 1973. NOTE: Although the original tempos for each song are listed, on the accompanying audio they are demonstrated at a slower tempo for instructional purposes.

I Can't Explain
(Single), 1965

The song was Townsend's reaction to the Kinks' hit, "You Really Got Me," which was released in early 1964. (The Who recorded "I Can't Explain" as their debut single at the end of 1964.)

The following transcription is taken from the pre-chorus. Though Moon wasn't known for his hi-hat playing, you can see that he used it quite effectively for off-beat openings in "I Can't Explain." Notice how he changes up his bass drum pattern and provides a hint of a twist beat in the fourth measure with snare hits on 4 and 4 +.

Groove 1

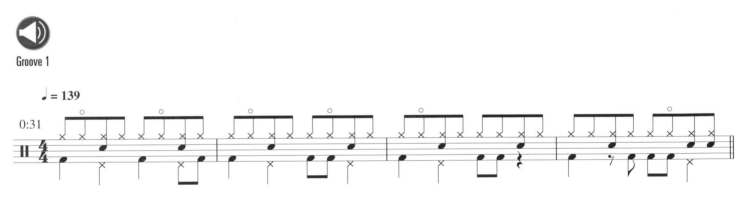

The Kids Are Alright
From *My Generation*, 1965

It may or may not be a coincidence that "The Kids Are Alright" was released later in the same year (1965) as a hit by another British band, "(I Can't Get No) Satisfaction"—a song with a similar groove by Charlie Watts of the Rolling Stones. Though Moon was likely influenced by Watts' beat, he was undoubtedly even more inspired by the original feel popularized by Motown in the early '60s—four quarter notes per measure on the snare, and the bass drum providing rhythmic interest. By playing his right hand on the ride instead of the hi-hat, Moon puts his personal stamp on the groove.

Groove 2

♩ = 139

0:05

The Ox
From *My Generation*, 1965

"The Ox" is an instrumental jam created spontaneously during the *My Generation* sessions. The song features frenzied piano by session ace Nicky Hopkins, a low-frequency guitar riff by Townsend, a bass lead by Entwistle, and surf-inspired drums. (Check out "Waikiki Run" off the Surfaris' album *Surfaris Play* for Moon's inspiration.)

The following passage is from the last six bars (out of a 12-bar form). Moon takes a "solo," though the rest of the band—except for the piano—is still playing. The 16th notes that Moon churns out during this improv are similar to what he plays over the entire tune, so it's hard to differentiate solo from groove.

Though Moon was known to use a four-piece (one rack tom and one floor tom) during this time, it sounds here as though he's using a five-piece (two rack toms and one floor tom). His snares are turned off to give him a high-pitched tom sound. With four tom sounds at his disposal, he creates the drum melody that you hear in "The Ox." Notice how he repeats each measure in these six bars notated here. Jazz drummers commonly use this concept to clarify each improvised statement for the listener.

Groove 3

♩ = 146

snares off

1:19

Substitute
(Single), 1966

Though "Substitute" only reached #5 on the British charts and wasn't particularly well received in America, it was a predictor of the great songwriting to come from the Who (and especially Townsend, who wrote this song and most of the Who's catalog). Moon was just beginning to develop his style. Here in the second chorus, he drives the beat with mostly consecutive eighth notes on the bass drum—a concept used in R&B music of that time. He also uses quarters on the snare to break up the backbeat and crashes into a ride cymbal to create wash over the top. The last two bars connect the chorus to the next verse; Moon changes course here by riding on the floor tom and playing a twist on the snare.

Groove 4

Baba O'Riley
From *Who's Next*, 1971

"Baba O'Riley" is another song from *Who's Next* that involves programmed synth, which was a novelty at the time. "The Who were the first band that I saw playing along with a sequence, and I thought it was very successful," recalls Henrit (drummer for Argent and The Kinks). Similar to "Won't Get Fooled Again" (analyzed and transcribed earlier in the book), Moon doesn't allow himself to be hamstrung by playing to a click. He shows off his funky, subtle side with four-stroke ruffs (sextuplets) and snare 16ths on the 2 *a*. Check out how Moon plays along with only one (not both) of Townsend's power chords per measure. Instead of hitting both 1 and 4, he comes down only on beat 1. Very few drummers possess this kind of taste and restraint.

Groove 5

Baby Don't You Do It
From *Who's Next,* 1971

By covering the Marvin Gaye Motown hit, Moon and the Who also paid homage to Bo Diddley (and the groove that he made famous on tunes such as "Hey! Bo Diddley"). This transcription is taken from the six-bar drum intro that very well might be Moon's reaction to John Bonham's intro from the Led Zeppelin song "Rock and Roll" (recorded only months before *Who's Next*).

Similar to the original Gaye drum part, Moon uses a contrapuntal concept on the drums: each sound source—crash, snare, and bass drum—play interesting rhythms on their own. When each component is then played together, it sounds like more than one drummer. A little bit of sloppiness only adds to the charm.

Groove 6

The Real Me
From *Quadrophenia*, 1973

Though not known for his funky drumming, Moon conjures up Mitch Mitchell in "The Real Me," playing a groove similar to "Fire" by The Jimi Hendrix Experience. In this eight-bar intro, off-beat bass drum notes, added snare drum quarters (in measures 2 and 3), and over-the-bar eighth/16th combinations between measures 3 and 4 all have an unsettling effect on the listener.

Groove 7

ESSENTIAL FILLS/SOLOS

"I didn't actually listen to drummers. I listened to riffs, and I play riffs on drums." [Keith Moon]

"Drum solos are the most boring, time-consuming things. I don't think the drums are a solo instrument. Drums are there to set the beat for the music." [Keith Moon]

Moon improvised so frequently, you often can't differentiate between what is a fill and what is a solo—and you don't really need to. His fills varied dramatically in length and oftentimes became entangled with the groove itself. His solos were mostly played over instrumental vamps (a concept used quite often in the jazz world).

Before you listen to and learn the following material, remember that Moon thought about his parts in different terms. To him, rock drumming was meant for more than just accompaniment. He put himself in the center of the fracas: directing traffic and lifting the music, while at the same time, imposing his will to express himself. NOTE: As with the Essential Grooves chapter, these examples are played slower than the marked tempo on the accompanying audio.

The Kids Are Alright
From *My Generation*, 1965

Moon plays a number of groundbreaking one- and two-measure fills, such as those at 0:33, 0:40, 1:22, and 1:29, but it's his 10-measure solo (really 14 bars if you count the additional four bars of connective tissue leading into the final verse), played over a guitar/bass vamp, that leaves you awestruck.

Though the vamp is mostly a power chord on beat 1, Moon adds additional crash hits on the 2 + and 4 (the "3 side" of a 3:2 clave). Listen to how he fills in the space between those hits in a variety of ways: sextuplets (including four-stroke ruffs as seven-stroke rolls), dotted eighth to 16th notes, and 16th/eighth combinations. Eighth-note hi-hat chicks help keep time in the first two measures, while eighth-note bass drum takes over throughout the rest of the solo. In the eighth measure, when Townsend and Entwistle change chords and begin playing eighth notes themselves, Moon changes course and bangs out a barrage of 16ths with his hands.

Fills/Solos 1

Substitute
(Single), 1966

The following three fill excerpts speak to the creative spark that Moon brought to the Who. Each phrase is gleaned from similar moments in the song, when Moon is given two bars of open territory. In the first example (0:58), he leaves space until a gutsy entrance on the 2 *a*. In the second example (1:48), Moon plays a twist beat with floor tom riding and consecutive bass drum eighths underneath. In the last example (2:36), one measure of rest is followed by a power flam eighth on the downbeat of the second measure and then 16ths around the drums.

I'm Free
From *Tommy*, 1969

According to Entwistle, he and Townshend teamed up to lay down a basic drum track to help Moon get over his confusion with the guitar riff that starts the song (the intro). Moon then "added all of the breaks."

"He was hearing it differently from how we were, and he just couldn't shake it off. So we put down the snare, the hi-hat, and the tambourine…When we did it live, the only way to bring him in was for Pete and I to go like this [makes an exaggerated high kick], which must have looked completely nuts." [Entwistle interview in *Drums & Drumming*]

A closer examination backs up most—but not all of Entwistle's story. A basic drum track (with tambourine) can be heard throughout the song, but it sounds like Moon laid down his own entire track (groove and fills) over the basic one (in other words, he tracked an overdub).

Fortunately for the listener, the fills are definitely Moon's, and they give the song essential boosts of energy. Two examples of this are shown here. At 1:00, he plays a short syncopated fill—completely unique from the rest of the song—starting on the 2 +. You'll notice a ton of sextuplet bursts interspersed throughout the song, but the two-bar phrase at 1:56 stands out because it uses both duplet (16ths) and triplet (sextuplet) half-measure fills.

Fills/Solos 3

See Me, Feel Me
(Single), 1970

"See Me, Feel Me" consists of two overture parts taken from the final song of *Tommy's* "We're Not Gonna Take It." The second part of the song, "Listening to You," is full of inspiring fills by Moon. Most of the licks are consecutive 16th-note flat flams played between floor and rack toms, contrasted by occasional sextuplet fills on the snare. He also offers up a number of syncopated flat flams. The notation here reveals three short fills (each one measure) and one long fill (three measures). Listen to how Moon contrasts the vocals in the first three examples and supports the vocals in the last example (final two beats).

Fills/Solos 4

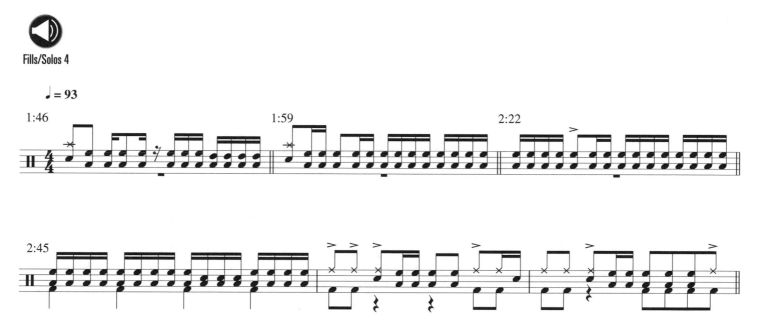

Baba O'Riley
From *Who's Next*, 1971

The one-measure phrase coming out of the bridge section of "Baba O'Riley" is one of the most air-drummed fills in rock history. What makes this lick so engrossing? The incredible tom sound? Driving eighth notes underneath? The three-over-four polyrhythm implied in the first two beats? The use of syncopation in the first half of the measure ending with a 16th flow in the last half? Chances are that Moon created the fill instinctively, and his only aim was to pump up the energy into the next verse.

Fills/Solos 5

In a Hand or a Face
From *Who by Numbers*, 1975

Moon and Entwistle often played off each other while creating fills. This is especially apparent in live performances, but "In a Hand or a Face" is a great studio example of this. In an interview published in *Drums & Drumming*, Entwistle was asked about whether this particular one-measure fill (which joins a Townsend guitar riff after three measures) was planned out or overdubbed. He replied, "No, neither. That's another example of the magic that can occur spontaneously."

Fills/Solos 6

This leads to a conclusion about Moon's fills and solos. He is a listener. He absorbs what he hears around him—often in the moment—and reacts, instead of creating art in a vacuum. Whether he contrasts, supports, or simultaneously copies (as he does in "In a Hand or a Face"), his genius stems from a team concept. In other words, the other members of the Who are just as responsible for these moments as Moon himself.

If you're in a band (if not, get in one immediately), you'll sound more like Moon if you use teamwork. Speak to your bass player and talk about a strategy for producing fills. Play together, leave space for one another, or contrast each other. You'll have more fun, and it might even sound better.

STYLISTIC DNA

In this section, we examine the building blocks of what contributes to Moon's style. Much of the material is extracted from watching hours and hours of live footage. Reoccurring themes were gathered and transformed into exercises. Though it's not possible to spend time observing Moon behind the kit, this chapter is, hopefully, the next best thing.

Coordination

"He used to hit the bass drum like you'd never seen. It was like a cannon, like a bomb going off when he hit it." [Teenage friend Gerry Evans referring to Moon's drum teacher and idol Carlo Little— from Tony Fletcher's book, *Moon*]

Though not known as a master of four-limb independence, Moon's level of coordination, developed mostly as a teenager, served him well throughout his career. The bass drum—and the bottom end that it puts out—became an important part of his style. In the following eight-bar exercise, rhythmic ideas often used by Moon are placed over continuous, eighth-note bass drum. Though the hand part is shown here on one surface (notated as a snare drum), feel free to experiment with orchestrating around the kit. Also, try simultaneous double-bass (assuming you have access to two bass drums or a double pedal) and left foot only (hi-hat chick and/or left-foot bass drum).

NOTE: Prescribed sticking is purposefully left out here. Moon often used right-hand lead (landing on each beat with the right stick) but was also helped out by his ambidexterity. In other words, he could comfortably start or finish a phrase with either hand. This also extends to coordination: Moon was at ease with his left hand hitting at the same time as his right foot (and vice verse).

DNA
Example 1

Dynamics

"For Christ's sake, play quieter," said the club manager. To which Moon replied, "I can't play quiet; I'm a rock drummer." [*New Yorker*, James Woods]

Though Moon was a proud member of one of the loudest rock bands in history, his dynamic control is what really stands out. His loud notes pop because of his effective use of surrounding softer notes and space.

Accenting

The following four-bar accent patterns often used by Moon are notated on one surface and then with accented notes placed around the drums.

DNA
Example 2

Crescendos

Moon uses crescendos to help transition one section of the song to the next. Here, snare 16ths are played soft to loud over the course of three measures, ending with a crash in the fourth bar. Make sure to increase the volume gradually over the three measures to prevent prematurely topping out.

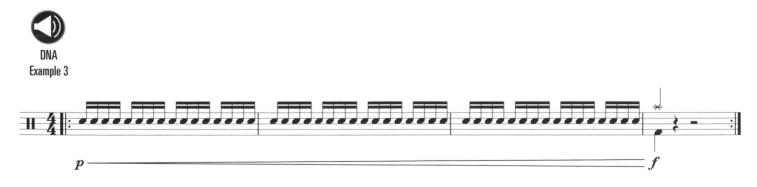

DNA
Example 3

Fill/Solo Elements

Random/Chaotic

Random-sounding fills and solos are a staple of Moon's risk-taking style. It may seem counterintuitive to write an exercise to help you create chaos. After all, what we're talking about here is moving your hands (and possibly feet) without much thought. Does the lack of structure make it possible to practice this "skill?" The answer is "yes."

In the case of a stream of 16th notes, the following tips will help you create random fills:
- Learn to count, feel, or hear what a specific number of 16ths sound like. In other words, if you first learn what one measure (four beats) of 16ths (1 *e + a* 2 *e + a* 3 *e + a* 4 *e + a*) sounds like, you're more likely to be able to cut that in half (two beats), in quarters (one beat), etc. You will be able to lay your sticks on a variety of drums and be confident of where you are when you come out of the fill.
- Odd numbers of hits on any one sound surface—especially one or three hits—sounds more random than even numbers of hits.
- Moon played mostly single strokes around the drums during his random runs, but used doubles (and paradiddles) as a means to pivot back in the opposite direction, therefore not needing to cross over.
- It sounds more chaotic if you vary the frequencies of the objects that you strike. For instance, hit a snare (high sound) and then follow it up with a floor tom (low sound).

This one-measure lick follows the tenets of chaos mentioned above. Sticking recommendations are included for ease of movement. Now go create some chaos.

DNA
Example 4

Anticipations

Many of Moon's fills started with his left hand on the snare drum. Though unusual for most drummers, it makes sense in two ways:
- The left hand is already on or near the snare from when you play backbeats.
- Most of the time that Moon did this, he was purposefully playing anticipations (defined as the rhythmic position before beats 1, 2, 3, and 4, such as the *4 a*). Starting the anticipations with your left allows your right hand to come down on the beat.

Starting fills slightly before the obvious spot is a concept used quite often in jazz but rarely in rock. Entwistle himself was baffled by this: "He went from the snare to the toms a lot, and he'd always start his breaks with his left hand instead of his right, which was sort of strange." [*Drums & Drumming*]

To get the hang of playing anticipated fills in the Moon style, one measure of groove is paired with four different snare fills. Again, feel free to exchange any snare notes with sound sources of your choice.

DNA
Example 5

Motions

Rock drummers often get caught in a trap of playing fills "down the drums," or from high to low. The motion is easy to pull off, and bandmates and audiences alike are used to the sound. Moon, however, didn't allow himself to be tied down by any conventions. He did execute fills from high to low but just as often used different motions. Entwistle recalled, "He didn't play from left to right or right to left [that's not exactly accurate]; he'd play forwards. I've never seen anyone play like that before or since." In other words, Moon would sometimes use the snare as home base, and venture out and back from there.

The following exercises give you four chances to try the forward and backwards motion so common in Moon's fills.

DNA
Example 6

Crash

Moon liked the sound of a crash (with or without underlying bass drum) to break up his licks. James Woods wrote in *The New Yorker*, "He delights in hitting his cymbals as often as possible and off the beat, rather as jazz and big band drummers do. The effect, of all these cymbals being struck, is of someone shouting out at unexpected moments while waiting in line—a yammer of exclamation marks." The following four-bar solo phrase includes a number of these high frequency explosions.

DNA
Example 7

Groove Elements

Because his unorthodox style came at a time when rock 'n' roll was still in its infancy (or at least in its toddler stage), the amount of opinions, misconceptions, and contradictions about Moon's playing style is pretty staggering. In fact, getting to the bottom of this is somewhat like a detective trying to solve a mystery. Did he have a deep pocket or not? Did he develop a lead drummer's mentality to better fit with what the rest of the band was doing, or did his style come from simply trying to feed his ego?

As it turns out, interacting with his bandmates—both on stage and in the studio—was the most important part of making music for Moon. "I just want to play drums for the Who, and that's it," he said. However, it's also apparent that he gave much of himself to the audience. He once explained, "I always go out with the intention of making 'em leave the theater saying, 'What a great drummer!' That's the way I think. I want the audience to like what I'm doing."

When Moon goes full tilt with sticks and feet flying in a seemingly random way, it can be a challenge to dig up the raw materials that make up his groove playing. Here are some tendencies that were uncovered and, hopefully, a few more tasty choices to add to your drop-down menu.

Four on the Snare

Use the following patterns to provide you more practice with the four on the snare concept that Moon uses in "The Kids Are Alright." Make sure that all of your notes line up to avoid unintentional flamming. Although Moon didn't necessarily use them in this way, quarter-note hi-hat chicks are included for increased challenge.

DNA
Example 8

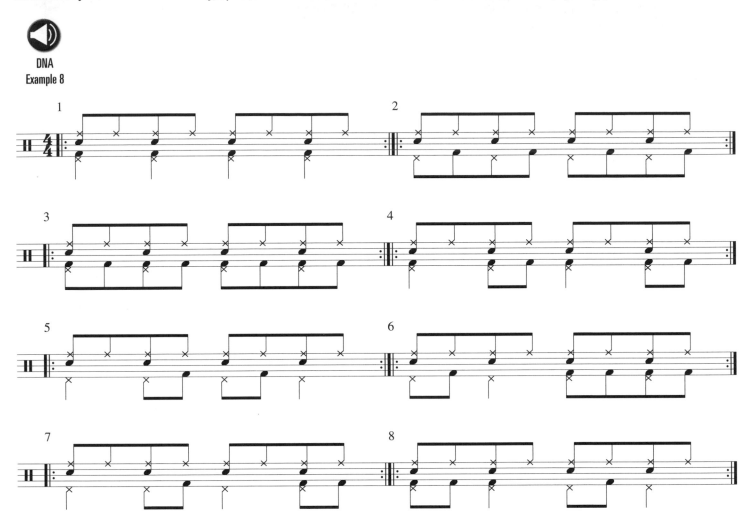

Crash Exchange

During wild musical moments, Moon would often move his right hand from one crash to another (and then continue to swing back and forth) while playing groove patterns. Though there is an obvious visual performance advantage by doing this, it's not clear that Moon made these sweeping movements for only that reason. This challenging motion is perceived by the audience as an uptick in energy level. Also, since each crash has a slightly different sound, the groove ends up sounding more interesting. Finally, by alternating, it gives each crash more time to decay than when you just ride on one crash. This creates complex, overlapping wash (resonance).

In the following exercise, a four-measure phrase is repeated. In the first two bars of each four-bar phrase, the right hand plays consecutive left-side crashes. In the second two bars of each phrase, the crashes alternate, either starting with the left-side crash or the right-side crash.

NOTE: If you don't own two crashes, substitute a ride cymbal for the right-side crash. Just make sure that you crash into the ride by using the shoulder/shank of your stick against the edge or crown of the cymbal.

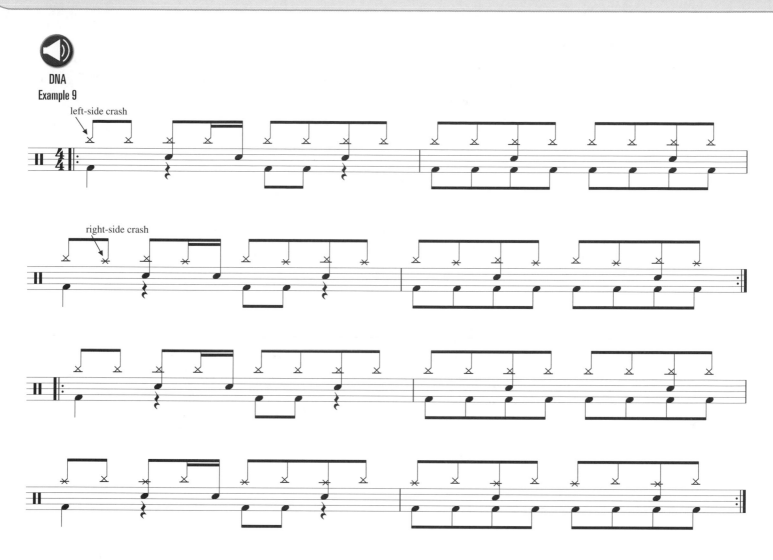

DNA
Example 9

Left-Hand Melodies

Possibly spurred on by Entwistle's adventurous bass lines or by the ever-increasing number of toms in his later drum kits, Moon began to use left-hand tom melodies in the middle of his grooves. This allowed him to further blur the lines between groove and fill and provide himself with yet another way to set up Townsend's famous power chords.

Four patterns are provided here—each gleaned from live performances—and feature the left hand traveling around the toms (and snare), while the right hand moves between the ride cymbal and the crash.

DNA
Example 10

Backbeat Displacements

From the very beginning of his career, Moon showed a penchant for moving his snare drum away from the typical backbeat position (beats 2 and 4). This may have been drawn out by Townsend's syncopated rhythm guitar and/or Daltrey's percussive vocal melodies. Maybe Moon simply got bored with playing backbeats over and over again.

Moon uses off-beats (the + of 1, 2, 3, and 4), and not the *e* and *a* of each beat (like funk drummers sometimes do). The following four patterns explore the way that Moon displaced the backbeat.

DNA
Example 11

Double-Bass Technique

When Moon switched from one to two bass drums around 1966, there is no evidence that he practiced to help with the transition. Though it's hard to believe that anyone could just sit down and play with his reckless abandon, Moon somehow pulled it off.

He did use the running method (fast single strokes between bass drums) to create big endings (along with cymbal rolls), but he rarely did this in the midst of a groove or fill. As you'll see in the following sub-categories, he developed some unusual ways to use double-kick. What's curious is that Moon influenced so many drummers to use two bass drums (or a double pedal) in their set-ups, but his double-kick techniques have gone largely unplayed.

Simultaneous Double-Kick

Moon used two bass drums at the same time—whereas other drummers would use one—to a most powerful effect. These four exercises are split between groove and fill/solo material.

DNA
Example 12

Left Kick Snare Matching

Moon often played his left foot on the kick simultaneously with his snare drum during groove playing. We can theorize that he did this out of habit, based on the time he played chick sounds with his hi-hat foot along with the snare. It's also possible that he just liked to beef up the sound of his backbeats. The following four patterns will get you started down this unusual path.

DNA
Example 13

Straight Eighths (Left)

Going one step further (sorry about the pun) with our theory that Moon transitioned his left-foot hi-hat chick technique into double-bass technique, the left foot plays consecutive eighth notes, while the right foot plays the more typical bass drum part. In the four exercises below, it's definitely all about the bass.

DNA
Example 14

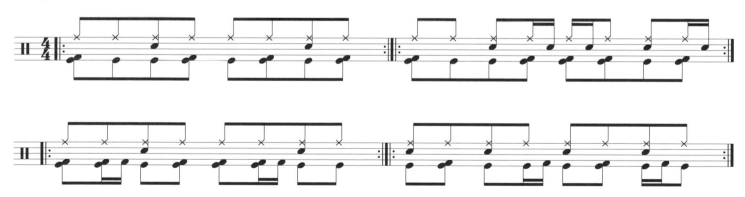

Four-Stroke Ruffs

As we've talked about extensively in the book, Moon loved the sound of the four-stroke ruff played as sextuplets. He often played the four notes with his hands and consecutive eighth notes on the bass drum underneath. Other times, he would play the first three sextuplets with his hands and finish with a final bass drum note. In the four examples here, we explore another four-stroke ruff orchestration: all notes played by bass drums.

DNA
Example 15

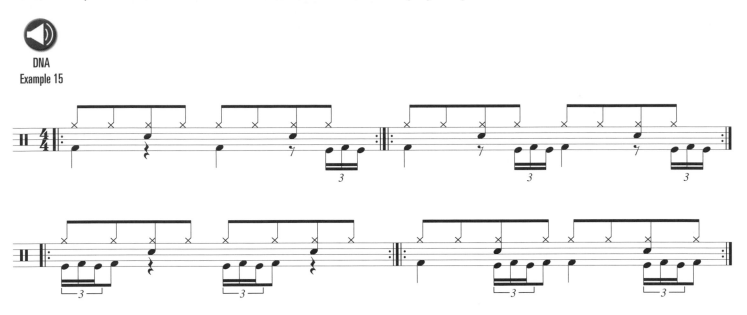

NOTE: Starting each four-stroke ruff with your left foot is probably the easiest option.

Left Side/Right Side

When his kits became larger and involved more and more toms, Moon developed a curious tendency: using his left-side bass drum while playing left-side drums and right-side bass drum while playing right-side drums. These two-bar exercises simulate Moon's roaming bass drum concept.

DNA
Example 16

Fall Where They May

At times while watching footage of the Who, it seems that Moon didn't have any predetermined strategy with his feet. He just let bass drum notes fall where they may. Though it's admittedly hard to replicate a wandering mind, the following four exercises will get you started.

DNA
Example 17

Creativity

"Pete would start an idea, and then we'd pick up on it until me or Keith would play a riff and start another idea. So you had these sort of islands to land on, and then we'd play off the top of our heads in between." [Entwistle interview, *Drums & Drumming*]

Moon is undoubtedly one of the most creative drummers in the history of rock. He listened and played off of the other members of the Who but was also unafraid to start the conversation. He was a master at controlling dynamics, orchestrating drums and cymbals, tapping into abstractions (see "Sense of Humor" later in this chapter), understanding song structure and coming up with parts that drive the music, inventing drum licks and grooves, and experimenting with his set-up to create new sounds. Though it's difficult to discuss what makes one drummer more creative than the next—and an even greater challenge to try to teach the concept—the following exercises might get you to think outside of the box.

Thinking Ahead

One of the secrets to improvisation is the ability to think ahead, so that you can relax in the moment. Moon never hesitated, so it's likely that he used this strategy quite often.

To do be able to pull this off, you will need to play a groove or fill while, at the same time, planning your next move. Here, we use the first verse of "Won't Get Fooled Again" as a simulation. Follow the provided road map in the notation and create your own groove pattern or fill when required.

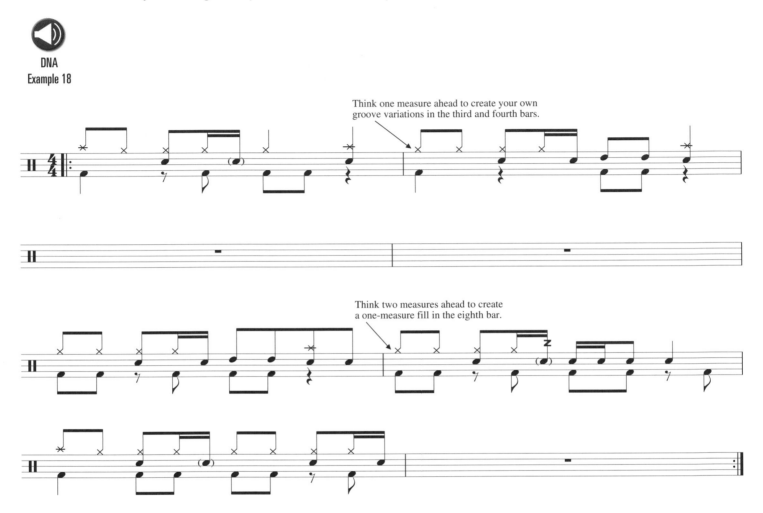

NOTE: Use *Playback+* from the accompanying audio and loop measures 26–33. Also, you will need to memorize or nearly memorize measures 1, 2, 5, 6, and 7 before trying this exercise.

No Hi-Hat

As you probably gathered from the Set-Up chapter, Moon was deeply into gear. He was one of the first rock 'n' roll drummers to use two bass drums and three rack toms and was known for his ever-growing, gigantic kits with multiple rows of toms and Latin/orchestral percussion.

On the flip side, Moon was also famously known for reducing his kit; in fact, for an extended period of time, he didn't use a hi-hat at all while playing live. Instead, he played time on crashes, ride, and floor tom only, and his left foot bounced on the ground or played a second bass drum. Limiting choices can not only make you focus on getting a lot of sounds out of one instrument but can positively affect creativity. Having to do more with less opens your mind to all kinds of possibilities.

In the following exercise, the crash cymbal is used for timekeeping purposes but played in four different ways: straight eighths, accented eighths, quarters, and with bass drum only. Notice how each treatment makes the patterns sound remarkably different.

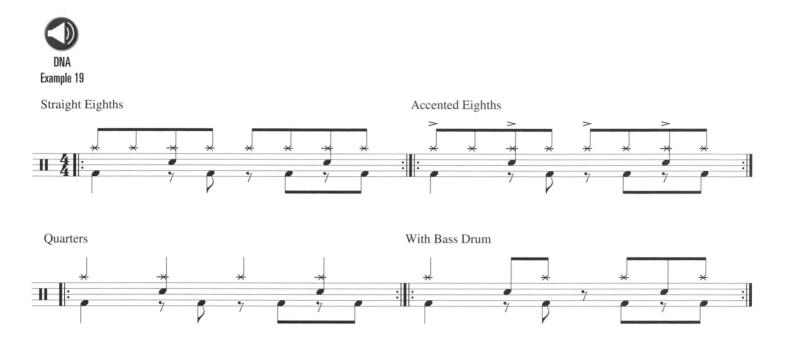

DNA
Example 19

NOTE: When riding on a crash, use the shoulder/shank of the stick against the edge of the cymbal to produce a washy sound. To play accented eighths, again use the shoulder of the stick for the accent but play the unaccented notes in one of a few ways:
- Tip of the stick on top of the cymbal.
- A glancing blow with the shoulder of the stick.
- Hitting the crown of the cymbal with the entire top portion of the stick.

To get the full Moon effect, bounce your left foot on the floor in time—either quarters or eighths. Also, you don't have to hit the crash cymbal with a great deal of force. Be careful to play dynamically balanced as Moon did. In other words, make sure that the cymbals don't drown out the rest of the kit.

Now, using *Playback+* from the accompanying audio, loop one chorus of "Who Are You." First, give yourself access to kick, snare, and hi-hats to create your own groove. Next, limit yourself by using kick and snare only (no hi-hats), bass and hi-hat only, and finally, just hi-hat.

Selective Listening

"The extraordinary thing about Keith is, whatever you think of him as a drummer...he listened." [Pete Townshend]

"We followed each other, but you have to remember, Keith played with everything. If you played his drum track alone in the studio, you just couldn't work out what song he was playing. Sometimes he played with the vocals, and you could tell that way." [Entwistle]

Creative musicians are almost always sensitive listeners, and it's not good enough to just listen earnestly. You need to hone your skills—as Moon did from the time he was a teenager—so that you can hear each and all of the instruments while you're playing. Listening only to yourself play may, in fact, ruin your chances at interacting with your bandmates.

Starting with the upcoming chapter, "Must Hear," or using any of the songs mentioned in this book, choose a section from a Who tune that uses drums along with bass, guitar, and vocals at the same time. For instance, the verse from "Bargain" would be a good choice.

Next, hone in on one instrument at a time, doing your best to block out the others. Pretend that the instrument you're focusing on is up close to you, while the others are far in the back of the room. Once you feel comfortable hearing each instrument separately, try to mentally pair two instruments together: drums and bass, drums and guitar, guitar and bass, etc. Now group three together. Finally, listen to the band as a whole, and you'll hopefully discover a changed perspective. Repeat the process again, but this time while playing the drums. This might take repeated attempts and increased concentration.

Contrast

Drummers can fall easily into a habit of copying what their bandmates do: matching the guitar riff, making sure your bass drum foot plays right along with the bass guitar, and accentuating the vocal melody. Moon certainly did his share of playing like this with the Who, but his contrasting moments might be more important to defining his style.

Using *Playback+* from the accompanying audio, loop measures 26–29 (the four bars right after the first verse) of "Pinball Wizard." Use the provided notation to play along. The first exercise shows what a typical drummer might play (matching the rhythm guitar), while the second is Moon's actual phrase (some matching, but mostly contrast) in the song.

DNA
Example 20

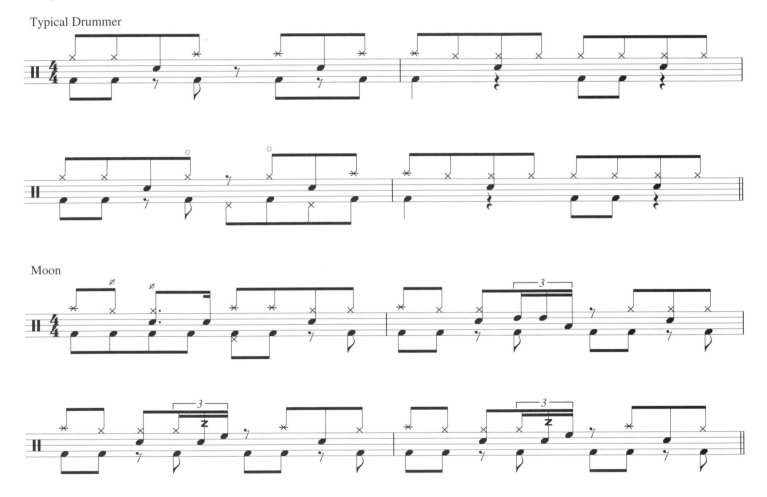

Next, create your own four-bar phrase to go along with the same segment from "Pinball Wizard."

Drummers—including Moon, of course—use contrast in solos and fills. As you contrast one phrase (or part of a phrase) with the next, it's as if you're having a conversation with yourself. On the drums, this is often done in two ways:

- **Rhythmically**: Fast rhythms are followed by slower ones (or vice versa), and busy or layered phrases are followed by simpler ones (or vice versa).
- **Sonically**: High frequency sounds, such as cymbals or the snare, are followed by low frequency sounds, such as a bass drum or floor tom (or vice versa).

The following exercise provides you with the experience of solo contrasting, both rhythmically and sonically.

DNA
Example 21

Sense of Humor

"He found out that if he played something silly, I could actually go with him and match it precisely. He became confident in that, so he played a lot of silly stuff." [Entwistle]

In interviews with Moon, it's obvious that he had quite a sense of humor. Because of his improvisational playing style, his comedic personality seeped into his drumming by quoting the rhythms of humorous melodies (or just making silly sounds). If you want to be able to play like Moon, you need to add some silliness into your style. Once you venture down this road, you may find it hard to fully return back to the land of the serious.

These four funny melodies are condensed down to one-surface rhythms. Do you recognize them?

1. Famous tag ending

2. "The Chicken"

3. "Benny Hill Theme"

4. "Jeopardy! Theme Song"

DNA
Example 22

Now play two measures of a rock groove followed by each of these two-measure fills. Try to come up with your own funny fills and see how your bandmates react to them.

NOTE: In the audio examples, the tempo is adjusted for each four-measure phrase to make each melody more recognizable.

MUST HEAR

Here is a short list of Moon's musical influences along with essential tracks from his extensive catalog.

Influences

Mainly Delaney by Eric Delaney and His Orchestra, 1957
Entire Album

Single—Gene Krupa with Benny Goodman and His Orchestra, 1937
"Sing, Sing, Sing"

Single—Elvis Presley, 1957 (Drums—DJ Fontana)
"Jailhouse Rock"

Single—Johnny Kidd & The Pirates, 1960 (Drums—Clem Cattini)
"Shakin' All Over"

Let There Be Drums by Sandy Nelson, 1961
"Let There Be Drums"

The Shadows by The Shadows, 1961 (Drums—Tony Meehan)
"See You in My Drums"

Surfaris Play by The Safaris, 1963 (Drums—Ron Wilson)
"Waikiki Run"

Single—Viv Prince, 1966
"Light of the Charge Brigade"

Career
(All by the Who except "Beck's Bolero" and Two Sides of the Moon)

"I Can't Explain" (Single), 1965

"Substitute" (Single), 1966

"Happy Jack" (Single), 1966

My Generation, 1965

Essential Tracks

"Out in the Street"
"I Don't Mind"
"La-La-La Lies"
"My Generation"
"The Kids Are Alright"
"The Ox"
"So Sad About Us"

A Quick One, 1966

Essential Tracks

"Run Run Run"
"Whiskey Man"
"Cobwebs and Strange"
"A Quick One, While He's Away"

"Beck's Bolero," 1967 (Single)

The Who Sell Out, 1967

Essential Tracks

"Heinz Baked Beans"
"Mary Anne with the Shaky Hand"
"I Can See for Miles"
"Medac"

Tommy, 1969

Essential Tracks

"Overture"
"Amazing Journey"
"Sparks"
"The Acid Queen"
"Pinball Wizard"
"Sensation"
"Sally Simpson"
"I'm Free"
"We're Not Gonna Take It"

Live at Leeds, 1970

Essential Track

Entire Album

Who's Next, 1971

Essential Tracks

"Baba O'Riley"
"Bargain"
"My Wife"
"The Song Is Over"
"Going Mobile"
"Behind Blue Eyes"
"Won't Get Fooled Again"
"Baby Don't You Do It" (New York Record Plant Session)

Quadrophenia, 1973

Essential Tracks

"The Real Me"
"Cut My Hair"
"5:15"
"Love, Reign o'er Me"

Two Sides of the Moon, 1975

Essential Track

"Crazy Like a Fox"

The Who by Numbers, 1975

Essential Tracks

"How Much Do I Booze"
"In a Hand or a Face"
"Squeeze Box" (Live)
"Dreaming from the Waist" (Live)

Who Are You, 1978

Essential Tracks

"New Song"
"Sister Disco"
"Trick of the Light"
"Who Are You"

MUST SEE

Seeing him in action—alongside drummers who were influenced by him or who have taken over his throne in the Who—will definitely clue you further into how Moon became one of the greatest drummers and entertainers in the history of rock.

On DVD

The Kids Are Alright, 1979

The Who Live at Royal Albert Hall (Zak Starkey), 2001

Amazing Journey–One Night in New York City (Mike Portnoy), 2006

Lambert & Stamp, 2014

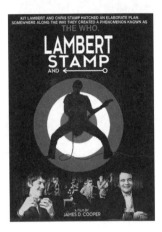

On YouTube

Use these search terms to find the following video clips.

Keith Moon Amazing Journey

Keith Moon Bio and Playing Style

The Who—I Can't Explain—Live on Shindig 1965

The Who—My Generation—Live 1965

The Who—Happy Jack—Live Performance on Beat-Club 1967

The Who—My Generation—Monterey Pop Festival 1967

The Who—Sparks—Tanglewood 1970

The Who—Wembley Stadium—Live Aid 1985 (Kenney Jones)

The Who—Who Are You—LA Second Set 1989 (Simon Phillips)

Jet Live—Cold Hard Bitch—Austin City Limits (Cris Cester)